'In *The Sanity of Belief,* Si_____ _____ _____,
quick wit and legal trainii _____ _____ r
or not there are strong eno _____ _____ e
through Christian faith. L_____ _____ _____, pimosopny, intera-
ture and more, his rapid-fire ideas come wrapped in a generosity
of spirit that leaves you feeling that he'd still be your friend
even if you disagreed with every word he said. This is a lively,
fresh and thoughtful exploration of Christian belief. Highly
recommended.'
Sheridan Voysey, presenter, BBC Radio 2's 'Pause for Thought', and
author of *The Making of Us: Who we can become when life doesn't
go as planned*

'Anyone who is interested in questions of meaning, significance,
goodness, truth, hope, love or suffering will find helpful insights
from a fellow traveller in this very readable book. Written by a
gifted thinker trained in law and theology, Simon Edwards shares
what he has discovered in his own journey, as he has worked
through difficult issues head-on, seeking truth based on credible
evidence. In the legacy of C. S. Lewis, he speaks to the ordinary
person in a humble, respectful and intellectually engaging manner
that is a pleasure to read.'
Thomas Tarrants, President Emeritus, the C. S. Lewis Institute

'Thought-provoking and exciting. This book invites you into a faith
that just makes sense.'
The Revd Canon Yemi Adedeji, author, pastor, speaker and Director
of One People Commission at Evangelical Alliance UK

'What's the purpose of life? Where can we find meaning and significance? How can we find hope in the midst of suffering? These are just some of the questions that all of us ask at some point in life, so how do we navigate our way through them and find answers that we can rely on? In this fantastically helpful book, Simon Edwards draws on his own personal story of wrestling with these questions to show why the Christian faith and the message of Jesus offer the most compelling answers to life's deepest questions. Beautifully and engagingly written, well researched, funny, moving and, at times, very personal, *The Sanity of Belief* shows why the Christian faith truly makes sense. Whether you're a seeker or a sceptic, or simply somebody who wants to follow Socrates' advice and avoid the unexamined life, this book will help you on your quest for not just the truth but also life in all its fullness.'
Andy Bannister, author, speaker and Director, Solas Centre for Public Christianity

'Simon Edwards has done us a great favour in writing *The Sanity of Belief*. He has drawn from the deep wells of human understanding – science, history, philosophy, Scripture and experience – to bring us something that is both clear and refreshing. His deceptively simple style is a pleasure to read and his wide-ranging case for the sanity of the Christian faith is convincing and satisfying.'
Dr John Dickson, author, historian and Distinguished Fellow in Public Christianity, Ridley College

'Many people believe that Christianity is irrational and irrelevant to real life. Simon Edwards, in his brilliantly written book, shows why this could not be further from the truth. *The Sanity of Belief* addresses the spiritual questions of this cultural moment in a unique and disarming way that appeals to reason and history as well as to humour and the ups and downs of everyday life. If you are not sure what you believe, this book is for you. If you do, this book is a must-read – and give it to your friends too.'
Sharon Dirckx, author and speaker, OCCA The Oxford Centre for Christian Apologetics

'Simon Edwards invites us to explore life's ultimate questions as an adventure. Powerfully argued and pleasingly written, this is a book for the open-minded and for the sceptic open to becoming more open-minded.'
Os Guinness, author of *Long Journey Home: A thinker's guide to the search for meaning*

'This book will help you to ask the right questions about life and its purpose.'
The Revd Les Isaac OBE, founder and CEO, the Ascension Trust

'Today, God is the great unknown. Many people reject a God who is merely the fruit of their imagination. Simon Edwards unveils this unknown God by presenting a strong case for the credibility and the sanity of Christian faith. Written with the accuracy of a lawyer and the passion of a lover, *The Sanity of Belief* is both thought-provoking and heart-warming. It provides seekers and believers alike with fresh water in a dry world, the water that meets our thirst for meaning and significance, the thirst for God.'
Pablo Martínez, psychiatrist and co-author of *Mad or God: Jesus, the healthiest mind of all*

'It is said that a good book is both an argument and a story. Simon Edwards offers both for those who appreciate a well-informed discussion of why the Christian faith makes sense. Written in an accessible style, this book invites the reader to consider fundamental propositions of faith. An engaging read that is cogently argued with the skill of a storyteller, the book draws widely from a variety of subject areas to construct the truism that faith in Christ really matters in our challenging times.'
The Revd Dr Sharon Prentis, Intercultural Mission Enabler and Dean of Black, Asian and Minority Ethnic Affairs, Church of England, Birmingham, UK

'What a riveting read. Honestly, there were moments when I felt like I was reading C. S. Lewis! Simon Edwards brings together the clarity of a legally trained mind, a tremendous grasp of theological and cultural ideas and the straight-talking approach of an Australian male! I assure you, as you read, the light will keep coming on.'

Rico Tice, Senior Minister, All Souls Church, Langham Place, London, and co-author of *Christianity Explored*

Simon Edwards is a Christian, husband and father to three kids. Born and raised in Australia, he worked as a lawyer before moving to the UK to study at the OCCA The Oxford Centre for Christian Apologetics and, later, the University of Oxford. He is now a writer and speaker at the OCCA and speaks regularly in the UK and abroad at conferences, churches, schools, workplaces and universities.

THE SANITY OF BELIEF

Why faith makes sense

Simon Edwards

First published in Great Britain in 2021

Society for Promoting Christian Knowledge
36 Causton Street
London SW1P 4ST
www.spck.org.uk

British Library Cataloguing-in-Publication Data
A catalogue record for this book is available from the British Library

ISBN 978–0–281–08489–0
eBook ISBN 978–0–281–08490–6

1 3 5 7 9 10 8 6 4 2

Typeset by Fakenham Prepress Solutions, Fakenham, Norfolk NR21 8NL
First printed in Great Britain by Jellyfish Print Solutions

eBook by Fakenham Prepress Solutions, Fakenham, Norfolk NR21 8NL

Produced on paper from sustainable forests

To
my beautiful wife and fellow adventurer,
Natasha

Contents

Contents

Introduction

Life is boring without any adventure. And some would say the most adventurous adventures are those of faith – adventures where there is a certain amount of risk involved in the venture.

When I was younger, I was a bit of an adventure seeker, but I was occasionally very reckless in my adventure seeking, as young men are prone to be. For example, when I decided rather impulsively to turn a mountain hike into a rock-climb across a 300-foot cliff without first checking for handholds (I needed to be rescued), or when I jumped off a precipice into quarry water below without first considering the height (my feet were so bruised I couldn't walk for days), or when I attempted to do a backflip on wet cement (an X-ray years later revealed a fracture in my neck).

Now, in hindsight, these things were not so much adventures of faith as adventures in stupidity. The difference between an adventure of faith and an adventure in stupidity is that the first is grounded in reason and reality, whereas the second is grounded in ignorance or delusion.

By way of illustration, many people join the Special Air Service (SAS) or the Navy Seals because they have a craving for adventure, and one of the things that you are required to learn in the special forces is how to skydive. There are plenty of people who would argue that you have to be mad to jump out of a perfectly good aeroplane, but according to the special forces, skydiving is neither an exercise in stupidity nor insanity. And that's because, as scary as it is to do, skydiving is grounded in reality. It is a well-thought-through, time-tested method of safely getting yourself from the back of a plane to a predetermined spot on the ground. Long story short, it works, and that's why the special forces use it.

But just because it works and is tested doesn't mean it doesn't take faith to do it. You have to overcome a fair amount of fear and self-protective instinct to trust in your parachute and your training and to finally jump out of the plane. But again, it is a reasonable trust because it's a trust grounded in reality and in experience. Skydiving without a parachute would be an act of insanity, whereas skydiving with a parachute is an adventure of faith. Scary, sure. But a reasonable faith, nonetheless.

We cannot go through life without faith. Without realizing it, we put our faith or trusting belief in all sorts of people (friends, family, doctors, teachers, chemists, mechanics, pilots, YouTube celebrities) and in all sorts of things (chairs, pills, textbooks, buses, lifejackets, stoplights and skin creams), just to name a few. Faith is unavoidable, but not all faith is equal. Trusting that the pills your chemist gave you aren't poisonous is reasonable. Skydiving with a special forces' instructor is scary but still reasonable. Bouldering across a 300-foot cliff without training or planning is just mad.

What about religious faith? Does it make sense to have faith in God? Some prominent atheists argue that belief in God is just a euphemism for 'insanity'. Sigmund Freud famously stated that belief in God is delusional. And more recently, in his book, *The God Delusion*, Richard Dawkins affirmed the view that: 'When one person suffers from a delusion it is called insanity. When many people suffer from a delusion it is called religion.'

Without doubt, Christianity calls people to an adventure of faith. But is it a reasonable faith, as Christians believe, if not a little scary; or nothing more than an adventure in delusion as these atheists suggest? To put it bluntly: is belief in God a form of insanity?

These are the questions this book is designed to address.

As a lawyer by background, I am interested in legal definitions. The traditional test of *insanity* in English law was established in a nineteenth-century case involving the attempted assassination of the then Prime Minister Robert Peel. In a case of mistaken identity, the assassin killed the PM's secretary, Edward Drummond. All agreed that the assassin, Daniel M'Naghten, was insane, but the question before the court was what constituted a valid legal defence of insanity. The judges decided that the test boiled down to these central questions: did the defendant know what he was doing, and if so, did he know that what he was doing was wrong?

Thus, under English law, someone who kills a neighbour because he or she believes that the neighbour is the devil would be deemed insane; but so, too, would be the person who kills a neighbour, knowing it is his or her neighbour, but not knowing that it is wrong to kill one's neighbour. In other words, an insane person can be someone who is completely out of touch with *physical* reality, but also someone who is completely out of touch with *moral* reality.

With that in mind, it is reasonable to assume that a sane belief is one that gives us a rational foundation for our belief in good and evil, right and wrong, as well as for our belief that the world around us is real and not just a dream or illusion. So, a sane belief is one that makes sense of and keeps us in touch with all of reality – both the moral and the physical.

Now, all of us lose touch with reality to some extent, from time to time, but this is not insanity. It is just a matter of diversion or distraction: we get glued to one aspect of reality and lose touch with the greater whole. For example, have you ever been on an aeroplane and found yourself lost in the drama of a really gripping film, only to be jolted back to the reality of the fact that you are currently situated at 30,000 feet above the surface of the earth and hurtling through the atmosphere at 600 miles an hour?

Such is the incongruity of international air travel. Headphones in, eyes glued to the screen in front of you, munching on pretzels and sipping on a drink kindly brought to you by an attendant at the press of a button – all the while doing something that people could hardly have dreamed of doing at the beginning of the previous century: flying.

When you think about it, it's really a rather incredible thing. I don't know about you, but whenever I let my mind turn away from the immediacy of the in-flight entertainment to the larger fact than I am *in flight* (and to all the countless instruments and components of a plane that need to be working in order to make this possible), I often feel butterflies in my stomach, as my mind attempts to comprehend the reality of my physical situation fully.

I find it's an apt metaphor for our lives and how easily we lose touch with the greater reality that is going on all around us. Consider for a moment how, when you are brushing your teeth in front of the mirror or scanning your emails on your phone, it is easy to take for granted, and even be oblivious to the fact, that the earth beneath your feet is spinning at roughly 1,000 miles an hour, while simultaneously hurtling us through the galaxy at 67,000 miles an hour. When you think about it, life is incredible, too.

I didn't ask to be born, and neither did you. Yet, here we are: breathing, thinking, feeling, experiencing, desiring, remembering, relating, planning, dreaming, hoping, fearing, loving, hating, waiting, wondering beings. Alive.

And even as we take our next breath, an uncountable number of things are happening in and around us, all at once, to make this possible. Things over which we have no control. Our heart is pumping blood through our arteries and veins; our brain is conveying information to the body's organs through its neural pathways; the atmosphere is providing our lungs with enough oxygen for us to live, while other gases it contains are shielding us from solar radiation; our planet is orbiting at just the right distance from the sun for life to exist; the moon is stabilizing the earth's axial wobble; our sun is radiating heat and light in a stable and enduring manner; the immense gravity of Jupiter is attracting rogue asteroids, comets and meteors away from the earth like a giant vacuum cleaner; and laws of motion, energy, matter and gravity are operating consistently across the quantum universe.

I'm feeling butterflies in my stomach again.

Now, it's not easy to retain conscious awareness of this reality in our day-to-day living, for two reasons. First, the inconceivably wondrous and precarious reality of our physical situation in the universe is almost too much for our minds to take in, let alone to hold on to, persistently.

But second, and more importantly, all this physical reality – as wonderful and precarious as it is – is merely the stage on which the drama of our lives is set. Our understanding of life would be incomplete if it never extended beyond the level of energy and matter, planets and gravity, brains and blood. Why? Because knowledge of these physical things, although it might help us stay alive, cannot much help us beyond that. It cannot help us with the decisions that really matter to us. Decisions about where we will live, or what we will do for a job, or whom we will love or trust or align ourselves with. It cannot help us decide what matters to us, nor can it inform us about the sort of person we are or should be, nor tell us how we should spend our days. Thus, our apprehension of reality must extend not only to physical realities, but to non-physical realities as well: to notions such as meaning, value, goodness, truth, hope and love, as well as their opposites. We might call them 'human' realities, for it is by them and in relation to them that we live and orient our lives. They are the things that really matter to us as human beings.

Sanity is about being in touch with all of reality. It implies wholeness or completeness across the full spectrum of human personality – intellectual, moral, relational, emotional and volitional. It is reasonable to assume, then, that a sane belief is one which is able to speak to and help make sense of reality in all its fullness – the physical and the moral; the scientific and the human – and without requiring us to leave our brains at the door.

A belief that not only helps us to understand the world around us, but also the world within us, including our deepest thoughts, intuitions, longings and emotions. A belief that makes sense, so to speak, both to the head and the heart. A belief that works in the real world.

Does Christian belief measure up to that test? Well, that is exactly what the rest of this book is designed to help us find out.

Part I

THE THINGS
THAT MATTER

1

The matter of meaning
What on earth gives my life meaning?

The unavoidable questions

A woman is working late again at the office, staring out her window at the familiar sight of the city lights. A young man is leaving his parents' home for the first time, entering into a brave new world of independence. An elderly woman is celebrating her eighty-fifth birthday, marvelling at how quickly the years have flown by. A farmer is gazing in awe, yet again, at the beauty of the night sky above. A philosopher is reading Plato in her leather chair. And a 14-year-old boy, in that strange midway point between childhood and adulthood, finds himself thinking about the future in a way he never has before. Different people. Different lives. But in the depth of their beings, they are all asking similar questions: what is my life all about? What is my purpose? How should I live? Where can I find lasting happiness?

By the way, that 14-year-old boy is me. Or at least, it was me.

It's not that I was in the habit of asking deep philosophical or spiritual questions back then. I grew up in a happy, ordinary, non-religious, Australian home. Conversations about God, religion, philosophy or the meaning of life were just not on the radar in any significant way. It wasn't that they were taboo, but for whatever reason, we never talked about them.

As a young teenager, what I was really into was sport. In fact, at one point in my teenage years, I was training in five different sports at the same time. I don't want to brag, but I was pretty good. I even made it to the national championships in athletics – though

3

few might guess that looking at me now! However, because I was training so much and growing at the same time, I ended up experiencing some significant problems with my knee joints, and the doctor said I had to cease and desist from all sports for the indefinite future to give my body time to heal. In that single moment, my lifestyle shifted from one of being very busy and active to one of having more time on my hands than I knew what to do with. I wouldn't have considered myself an overly reflective person, but with all this extra spare time, it got me thinking about life.

I can still remember the moment. Standing in the school playground at lunchtime and wondering to myself: if all life amounts to is that we live for 80 or 90 years and then we die and that's it – game over – and whatever we have achieved, whatever we have loved and whatever we have become will eventually and inevitably disappear into dust, well, I thought, not only is that a pretty sad story, it is also a meaningless one. Rather like a video game where no matter how well you play or what choices you make, it is always the same end result, every time. Blank screen. You lose.

And I remember thinking: 'That just doesn't feel like the right story. I wonder if it really is the right story. Because if it is, what's the point of it all?'

Rarely do we articulate questions like these out loud or to each other. I certainly didn't. Of course, life is busy. Each day is full of one hundred smaller little questions and challenges to solve. And in our leisure time, we have such an array of fully wired, stimulating entertainment options with which to fill and distract our minds that these deeper questions of the heart rarely find a space to surface.

But the questions are important. They are as old as humanity – like bread, or fire, or the wheel – and like these ancient things, they remain perpetually relevant as timeless human needs.

Case in point. If you had to choose a group of people in the world of whom it could be said that they seem to have everything in life one could possibly ask for, a good example might be undergraduate students at Harvard University, one of the leading universities of the world. They are young, gifted and with a world of opportunity at their feet. And yet, what do you think is the most popular course on campus? It is a course about how to find happiness called 'The science of happiness'. Psychologist Dr Ben-Shahar, who teaches the course, says the quest for happiness has always been an innate human yearning, dating back to the times of Confucius and Aristotle. When asked why his course is so popular among future elites who already have so much going for them, he attributes its success to the growing desire of these young people to make their lives more meaningful.

If Dr Ben-Shahar is right, then it is not youth, wealth, intelligence or achievement that brings happiness, it is meaning.

Life examined

The great seventeenth-century French thinker Blaise Pascal wrote: 'I have often said that the sole cause of man's unhappiness is that he does not know how to stay quietly in his room', suggesting to me that the main reason people don't find lasting happiness is that they don't give themselves the necessary time and space required to think deeply about the big questions of meaning and purpose. If that was true in Pascal's day, how much more must it be true in the age of the Internet and social media?

Socrates made a similar point when he famously said: 'The unexamined life is not worth living.' Mark Twain perhaps said it best of all when he observed: 'The two most important days in your life are the day you're born and the day you find out why.'

I have sometimes heard people, who consider themselves practical, dismiss such talk about meaning and purpose in life as too abstract and philosophical, yet there are few things in life of more practical importance. A Jewish psychologist by the name of Victor Frankl discovered this truth in a concentration camp during the Second World War. While contemplating how to survive the immense challenges of his imprisonment, Frankl began observing his fellow prisoners in the hope of discovering what coping mechanism worked well. He discovered that it was those individuals who could not accept what was happening to them – the ones who could not find a meaning greater than their present sufferings – who despaired, lost hope and eventually gave up and died. Conversely, those individuals who could find a purpose in life or a hope for the future beyond their present ordeal were far more likely to survive.

'He who has a "why" to live can bear with almost any "how"', wrote the philosopher Friedrich Nietzsche. Having meaning is essential to living, it is like oxygen for the soul. Sadly, it's often not until life hits some sort of crisis point that we eventually find ourselves (unavoidably) grappling with these big questions of life and its meaning.

Bestselling author Philip Yancey hit such a point when his car missed a bend on a winding road in Colorado and tumbled over the edge. He woke up to find himself strapped, head and body, to a hospital bed. A CAT scan showed that a vertebra high up in his neck had been shattered, and sharp bone fragments were protruding right next to a major artery. If the artery were pierced, he would bleed to death. During that time of waiting, knowing he might die at any moment, he called people close to him knowing it was perhaps the last time he would speak to them. He writes:

As I lay there, I realised how much of my life focussed on trivial things. Trust me, during [that time of waiting] I did not focus on how many books I had sold, or what kind of car I drive (it was being towed to a junkyard anyway) or how much money I had in my bank account. All that mattered boiled down to a few basic questions. Who do I love? Who will I miss? What have I done with my life? Am I ready for what's next?

This book is written with the belief that life should not be taken for granted; that we shouldn't wait for crisis points to live an 'examined life' and that if we really want to find lasting happiness, it is necessary that we grapple with the truly big questions of life. Questions like the following: in a universe far larger than our finite minds can sensibly comprehend, what gives our lives meaning? In a world of over seven billion people, what makes me significant? On a planet teeming with life of incredible complexity and beauty, are we all here by accident or design? With so many decisions to make each day, week, month and year, does my life have an overarching point or a purpose? Is there a hope I can hold on to in the midst of sickness and suffering and death?

Something more?

Perhaps the most famous story in the history of philosophy is that of Plato's cave. The philosopher asks us to imagine three prisoners in a cave, their bodies bound and their heads tied so that they cannot look at anything except the stone wall in front of them. They have been bound like that from birth, staring at that wall. They have no idea there is a world outside that wall, let alone outside the cave. A fire is burning behind the prisoners; between the fire and the prisoners, there is a walkway where people walk and talk and carry objects. The prisoners perceive only the shadows of the people and things passing by on the walkway as they are cast onto the wall. The prisoners hear echoes of the talk coming from the shadows. For the prisoners, the shadows and the echoes are reality. This is their world. Shadows and echoes. It is the only reality they know.

How, we wonder, might these people come to know that there is a better world than their shadow-world: a world of sunlight, blue skies and fresh air? Could something in the cave, or perhaps even the shadows and echoes themselves, come to be seen for what they truly are, not the ultimate reality, but clues or pointers to something beyond themselves? A deeper, fuller reality?

Or might these sorry occupants of the cave have an intuition that somewhere there is more to life than this drab and dull world they have always known? Perhaps they experience a deep sense of restlessness and dissatisfaction, a profound longing or hunger for another world – a reality they have never seen but which seems to haunt their thoughts and hopes, nonetheless?

This hunger for something more, something hard to define, something perpetually beyond our reach, is something that many people today identify with in their own lives.

I once spent a week speaking to some very smart and sophisticated people in a number of investment banks and consultancy firms in London on some of the big questions of life, and this same issue came up in question time and conversations – this shared intuition or hunger among people, who are outwardly very well off and successful, that there must be something more to life than simply that which this material world has to offer.

C. S. Lewis, the renowned Oxford don (whose writings I have found so very helpful, as you will notice by the many quotes of his scattered throughout this book), calls this hunger or desire the secret signature of every human soul: this sense, this longing, this hope for something that life cannot seem to provide but which we continue to hear echoes of in the depths of our soul; sometimes faintly, sometimes powerfully.

The philosopher Roger Scruton observes that no matter how prevalent atheism might become, as human beings we will always 'hunger for the sacred, the spiritual'. It raises an interesting question: if atheism is right, and if reality is nothing more than physical things playing themselves out in accordance with the inexorable laws of physics and chemistry, like one big machine, then why do we, who are a part and a product of this great machine, have longings for something more than the machine? And why is it that throughout history, from before the time of Plato and right up to and including today, so many people have acknowledged that there is a spiritual reality?

Could it be because a human being is actually more than just the sum of its parts; more than just meat and bones and chemicals? Interestingly, that's what Jesus of Nazareth believed and taught. As he famously said: 'Human beings cannot live on bread alone' (Matthew 4.4, TEV). By this he meant there is a spiritual dimension to who we are that physical things just cannot satisfy. And just as our physical hunger points to the existence of that which can satisfy our physical hunger, so too our spiritual hunger points to the existence of that which can satisfy our spiritual hunger.

Jesus also said: 'I am the bread of life. Whoever comes to me will never go hungry and whoever believes in me will never be thirsty' (John 6.35, NIV). In other words, 'That which can satisfy your spiritual hunger is me,' says Jesus. 'I am the bread that satisfies your soul.'

Now, if you are a staunch atheist, cut from the same cloth as, say, the atheist writer Richard Dawkins, you might regard belief in the existence of any spiritual dimension to reality as ridiculous and superstitious – a completely irrational faith.

A few years ago, Dawkins and the British Humanist Association sponsored an advertising campaign on the side of buses in London with the following slogan: 'There's probably no God, now stop worrying and enjoy your life.' Leaving aside the fact that his exhortation to stop worrying rests on the rather worrying word 'probably' (Dawkins could not rationally claim there is no God for, as he knows, to know with complete certainty there isn't a God would require an omniscience only God, if he existed, could possess), it is interesting that Dawkins assumes that worrying is to be equated with God's existence and enjoyment with his non-existence. But why? Particularly, when there are many who testify to having found deep satisfaction and fulfilment in a relationship with a God who loves them.

However, if one does believe the atheist vision of reality is true, that there is no God or any spiritual dimension to life, then what do we do with our deep hungers for meaning and for purpose?

According to a video entitled 'How can I be happy?' narrated by the well-known atheist and presenter and writer Stephen Fry, meaning is not to be found in any sort of divine plan or cosmic purpose to the universe but, rather, in the meaning we create for ourselves, which, he says, can be in anything that we choose, including, for example, in a commitment to politics, our career or some artistic endeavour; or just in simple pleasures such as drinking wine with friends, hiking in nature or tending to a garden.

Is that true? Do you agree? Do you think meaning can be found in the many and varied good things life has to offer, without life as a whole having any greater meaning or purpose behind it?

Chasing after the wind

An ancient Jewish philosopher, known as the 'Preacher' or 'Teacher', grapples with this very question in his book, Ecclesiastes, one of the wisdom books of the Hebrew Scriptures. Traditionally, this philosopher is held to be the famous and exceedingly wealthy King Solomon.

As the book opens, we are confronted with its most iconic phrase: 'Vanity of vanities . . . all is vanity and a striving after the wind' (Ecclesiastes 1.2, 14, ESV). Or in another translation: 'Meaningless! Meaningless!' says the Teacher. 'Utterly Meaningless! Everything is meaningless' (Ecclesiastes 1.2, NIV).

Not a very promising beginning. But this is the conclusion that the Teacher comes to after reflecting deeply about the human quest for meaning and fulfilment in life *under the sun* (a phrase which means something like 'without reference to any divine or cosmic purpose'). Like Dr Ben-Shahar, the professor who runs the course on happiness at Harvard, Solomon believes that people who reject any divine or cosmic purpose to life typically try to find meaning and fulfilment in one of two ways. Either in the pursuit of pleasure and experience or, for those who are able to discipline themselves and their desires, in the pursuit of success and achievement. Solomon thoroughly explores and examines both of these fulfilment-seeking pathways.

As a king, Solomon had access to the finest sensual and sensory pleasures on offer: the best of wine, women and song. He writes: 'I denied myself nothing my eyes desired; I refused my heart no pleasure' (Ecclesiastes 2.10, NIV). It sounds wonderful, but Solomon ultimately discovers that pleasure alone, no matter how good, just doesn't satisfy. In a society that tends to equate happiness with the absence of pain and an abundance of pleasure, that may seem surprising, but the testimony of many a pleasure-seeker is that in the long run, the highway of hedonism leads either to brokenness or to boredom. As the decadent Queen Marie Antoinette ruefully observed, eventually 'nothing tastes'.

'Meaninglessness does not come from being weary of pain, meaninglessness comes from being weary of pleasure', remarked the essayist G. K. Chesterton. It sounds counterintuitive, but it is true: pleasure's diminishing returns, far from providing an adequate foundation for fulfillment, only serve to highlight the sense of emptiness and boredom that come from a life devoid of any deeper purpose.

Therefore, Solomon also tries to find fulfilment in that other well-worn path, the pursuit of achievement and success. He commissions great public projects, builds houses, plants vineyards, designs gardens and parks, and constructs great reservoirs. He also acquires more wealth than anyone before him: herds and flocks, gold and the treasure of kings and provinces. He becomes greater in power, fame and status than everybody else. He writes: 'My heart took delight in all my labour, and this was the reward for all my toil' (Ecclesiastes 2.10, NIV).

And yet, despite accomplishing all this, in the end, he writes: 'when I surveyed all that my hands had done and what I had toiled to achieve, everything was meaningless, a chasing after the wind; nothing was gained under the sun' (Ecclesiastes 2.11, NIV).

As Solomon reflects on all his accomplishments, he concludes that whether one achieves very much or very little – or whether one becomes rich or poor, powerful or powerless, famous or unknown, in the end it doesn't matter, for all meet the same fate anyway. Life itself is an endless cycle where, as he puts it:

> Generations come and generations go . . . What has been will be again, and what has been done will be done again . . . No one remembers the former generations, and even those yet to come will not be remembered by those who follow them.
> (Ecclesiastes 1.4, 9, 11, NIV)

Thus, having found meaning in neither pleasure nor achievement, he finally tries to find it in wisdom, the last great consolation of the philosopher (Solomon is famous for writing many wise sayings). However, even wisdom fails to bring the desired meaning he hopes for. He observes that although it is better to be a wise person than a fool, and to walk in light rather than darkness, nevertheless the same fate comes to both the wise and the fool: 'For of the wise as of the fool there is no enduring remembrance, seeing that in the days to come all will have been long forgotten. The wise dies just like the fool!' (Ecclesiastes 2.16, ESV)

In short, Solomon concludes that the transience of our individual lives, combined with the endless cycle of history repeating itself *ad infinitum* throughout the ages because there really is, as he famously says, 'nothing new under the sun' (Ecclesiastes 1.9, NIV), leads to an inevitable sense of meaninglessness and boredom *under the sun*.

This sense of despair you feel by reading Solomon's take on life *under the sun* (that is, without reference to any divine or over-arching purpose) reminds me of the sense of despair I felt when I first came across an oft-quoted line by the well-known atheist philosopher Bertrand Russell, describing his take on life's big picture. Russell writes:

> Man is the product of causes, which had no provision of the end they were achieving. His origin, his growth, his hopes, his fears, his loves and his beliefs are but the outcome of accidental collocations of atoms . . . no fire, no heroism, no intensity of thought and feeling, can preserve an individual life beyond the grave . . . and all the labours of the ages, all the devotion, all the inspiration, all the noon-day brightness of human genius is destined to eventual extinction in the vast death of the solar system . . . the whole temple of Man's achievement must inevitably be buried beneath the debris of a universe in ruins . . .

That is the atheist story of life – the only sensible story to believe; or so we are told: forget all this talk of God or of any higher meaning to life, for life 'under the sun' is the only life there is.

But if that's true, what on earth makes your life or my life meaningful?

My story

That was the question I was really asking myself as a 14-year-old boy. What makes life meaningful? Around the same time as my hiatus from sport was causing me to think more deeply about life than I ever had before, I found myself being forced to sit in religious education classes at school because it was part of the curriculum. And in those classes I was being presented with a different story to the atheist story – one that says that we're not here by accident, we are here on purpose because somebody (God) wanted us to be here, and he loves us. I learned that the Bible teaches that God loves us so much that even when we walked away from God, instead of abandoning us, he reached out to us. And that in Jesus, God became one of us, entering into our world and dwelling among us, even dying for us on a Roman cross, to rescue us from the mess of selfishness we are in. And as I listened to this alternative story, the interesting thing was that, although the teaching was not delivered in a particularly engaging way, this story somehow seemed or *felt* more real or true than that other story: the one that was telling me that you and I are merely cosmic accidents in a universe of blind and indifferent forces, here through a random combination of time plus matter plus chance, that we live for a few decades if we are lucky, and then we're gone, for ever.

But feelings are one thing, facts another. I have always been much more of a thinker than a feeler, somewhat sceptical by nature, always willing to challenge a statement or an assumption with a demand for reasons and proof (which used to annoy my mother a lot, but also meant she wasn't at all surprised when I eventually became a lawyer). One day in the religious education class I attended, the teacher showed us a video production of a courtroom drama. But in this drama the Christian claim about the resurrection of Jesus was on trial, and incredibly (at least to my limited knowledge of Christianity), the defence was able to provide a compelling case for the resurrection. Now this was fascinating to me, the idea that there could be evidence for Jesus that could be investigated, the notion that there might be some substance to this thing called Christianity; this thing which had somehow moved me to *feel* that God might actually be real, that we might not be here by accident at all, and that death might not be the final chapter in everyone's story.

And because I now had plenty of extra time on my hands, thanks to my knee injuries, I began to investigate. I started going to the library at lunchtime. I started reading books – we didn't have the Internet back then, of course. I read books about different religions, books about different worldviews, books about the relationship between belief in God and science, philosophy and history, and over a period of months, I came to the conclusion that of all the various explanations as to why it is that we find ourselves in this incredible universe that we do, Christianity is by far the best explanation on offer. In short, the Christian version of the story made sense to me; more sense indeed than all the alternatives, including atheism.

For example, I couldn't swallow the atheist view that we must simply regard the universe as a brute fact (a fact that has no explanation). It seemed to me that there were so many interesting and unlikely aspects to the universe – things such as music, mathematics, love, consciousness, our longings for eternity and the sheer unlikelihood of life – that it really begged an explanation.

Or for example, I remember being attracted to the New Age or age-old Eastern mystical idea that the answer is within me, that deep down I am really a divine being, but then feeling that, as attractive as this idea sounded, it simply did not accord with my experience of myself. I certainly did not feel divine and, if I was truly divine, how was it that I had somehow forgotten that I was?

Moreover, I remember coming to the realization that various religious beliefs I read about had one thing in common: they seemed to me to suggest that if I thought the right thoughts or did the right things or practised the right spiritual activities, I could work or earn my way towards heaven or Nirvana or God or salvation or whatever it was that that particular worldview or philosophy was offering – except one. Christianity alone stood out in stating,

15

in no uncertain terms, that there was nothing I could do to help myself. Rather, it taught that I needed to be saved. I needed 'spiritual resuscitation'. It said that we could never work our way up to God by moral performance and that we didn't have to because God had come down to us, in Jesus Christ, to do for us what we could not do for ourselves. And I remember thinking, as a 14-year-old, that this did not seem like a story invented by human beings because it went completely against our natural human instinct to want to prove ourselves somehow and to demonstrate how good we are, an instinct to which I could very much relate as a competitive young man.

These are but some examples of the 'ring of truth' that Christianity seemed to me to possess. No one reflection was in itself conclusive that Christianity was true, rather, it was the gradual accumulation of many reflections, insights and pieces of evidence, taken together, that increasingly suggested to me that Christianity made sense. And so it was that through this process of reading and thinking, investigating and reflecting, I eventually came to the intellectual conclusion that Christianity was indeed true. My instincts that we aren't all here by accident, that life does have meaning, that there really is a right and a wrong way to live and that death is not the final reality for a human being, found for themselves a solid grounding in the Christian understanding of reality.

Don't get me wrong, however. Even though it was primarily my intuitions about life that initially caused me to doubt the atheist version of reality, I was willing in my investigation to go wherever the evidence led me. And if the evidence had led me to the conclusion that the atheist story was true and that death and nothingness is the ultimate end for everyone, no matter how well they play the game of life, well then, I would have been willing to swallow that hard truth. I would have still tried to find pleasure and happiness in whatever time was allotted to me. But I couldn't have believed, as some atheists are able to believe, that life was still meaningful.

What I would have said is: although it feels as if it is meaningful, in the cold hard light of logic, I must admit, it really isn't. Because if, in the eternal scheme of things, the choices that I make in life make no difference to my ultimate outcome, and nothing we do in this life endures or has any lasting value, then I have no rational basis upon which to call my choices or actions in life meaningful or 'of consequence'. However, as I investigated the evidence (from science, history, philosophy, human experience and the Bible), it led me to conclude that it was atheism that was wrong about life, not my intuitions.

But that wasn't the end of my journey of discovery. A number of weeks later, I noticed one of my classmates reading a little green booklet in the playground. I asked him what it was and he simply said, 'here, have it', then he gave it to me and walked off. I found his behaviour rather puzzling, but when I looked at the booklet, I discovered it was a little tract explaining why Christianity is good news. In essence, it said: God made you, he loves you, but all the wrong things you have done have separated you from God. But the good news is that God sent Jesus into the world, not to condemn us but to rescue us, and through this Jesus – who died for us on a cross and rose again – we can experience forgiveness and peace with God now and for all eternity, as we entrust our lives to him.

At the end of that little booklet, I was presented with a choice. Do I want that? Am I willing to entrust my life to Jesus and follow him, in the way that an apprentice follows in the footsteps of the master craftsman? Was I willing, as it were, to bend my knee to him as Lord and as Saviour of my life?

This little booklet, along with the decision it presented to me at the end, crystallized for me this important truth: being a Christian involved more than just believing that God exists; it was also about believing what he says and acting accordingly. In other words, it was about following him. But by this stage, choosing to follow Jesus was actually something I was all too willing to do because by then, I had not only come to believe that he was real and that he was good, I had also come to love him, for I had come to understand, through reading the Bible, just how much he loved me.

That's my story, and of course, the story continues. But as I said, it all began with the question: what makes my life meaningful?

Irrelevant, irrational and immoral?

Of course, a lot of people today would argue that Christian faith is irrelevant, irrational and possibly even immoral. Sometimes people have this view because their picture of Christianity is different from the real thing, merely a caricature based on what they have heard about Christianity and which actually isn't true. I have often found myself in conversation with people in which my response has been: 'I don't like the God you are talking about either, but then the God you are talking about is not the God of the Bible.'

Other times, however, people have come to negative views about God or the Bible because they have good questions or reasonable objections to some aspect of Christian belief or teaching to which they have heard no good answer. I'm hoping that this book, as well as giving good reasons for why a person would believe what Christians believe, might also address some of the heartfelt concerns and intellectual objections that people have about Christian faith. And I acknowledge that many of the questions to be addressed are profound and challenging indeed.

The approach I take in this book assumes that if we are truly to find meaning in life, then the following things about our lives need to be true: first, that who we are matters – which is a question of value. Second, that what we do matters – which is a question of goodness. Third, that what we experience is real – which is a question of truth. Fourth, that our relationships are meaningful – which is a question of love. And finally, that we need to be able to make sense of the greatest challenge to hope and meaning in this life – which is the question of suffering.

Meaning, value, goodness, truth, love, hope and suffering. These are the things that matter. For these are the questions we must grapple with as human beings if we are to make sense of life and find satisfaction for our souls.

2

The matter of value

What makes me special in a world of seven billion?

Some things in life are special

One fine day in California in 1967, a woman, on her evening walk, stumbled across a violin that had apparently been abandoned on the side of the road. She decided to take the instrument home and, not playing the violin herself, gave it to her young nephew. Her nephew was not very interested in the violin but gratefully accepted it anyway as any good nephew would. So, the violin remained with the boy, who grew up and eventually married. His wife, when she discovered the violin, decided that she would like to learn to play it. That woman's name was Teresa Salvato. So, Teresa started taking lessons, and then one day in the spring of 1994, 27 years after the violin had been found by the side of the road, Teresa decided to take the violin to a repairer for a tune-up.

If somebody had asked Teresa how much the violin was worth, she would have replied that she had absolutely no idea. The reason she had no idea of the value of the violin was because she didn't know anything about it. But the violin repairers quickly realized that the violin Teresa had brought in was not an ordinary one. It was a very special instrument. So special, it even had its own name. The name of the violin was 'The Duke of Alcantara'; for that was the name which had been given to the violin 267 years before by the person who had made it, a man by the name of Stradivarius! Teresa had no idea that the violin on which she had been learning to play was a Stradivarius and worth over a million dollars. And found on the side of the road.

Apparently, it had landed there because in 1967, the second violinist of the orchestra of the University of California had pleaded to use the violin in a concert and, well, have you ever put something important on the roof of your car and then accidentally driven off, forgetting you had put it on the roof of your car? It appears that's what the second violinist did with the Stradivarius violin.

Stradivarius violins remind us that some things in life are special. Some things in life are significant. Some things in life require us to treat them with care and dignity. But what is it that makes something significant? What is it that makes something valuable and special? In short, what is it that makes *you* special? In a world of seven billion people, what makes your life significant? What gives you value?

We can know the value of a violin based on the identity of the instrument. And we can know the identity of an instrument based on its origin. Could it be the same for us? If so, then our value as human beings cannot be understood without reference to our true identity. And our identity cannot be understood without reference to our ultimate origin.

But if this is true, what happens if we lose connection with our identity (who we really are) and our origin (where we really came from)? What then provides the framework for our understanding of human dignity and essential worth if, as society is increasingly doing, we remove God from the picture?

For the atheist who believes that there is no creator God, and there is nothing more to reality than a purely physical universe, everything we are, everything we do, everything we think and feel, is – fundamentally – just physical processes playing themselves out in a complex system of cause and effect. According to the renowned psychologist and atheist B. F. Skinner, 'Man is a

21

machine.' A complex machine, of course but, in the end, simply a machine. In that respect his behaviour is completely determined in accordance with physical laws in operation.

One is tempted to respond to this assertion by asking why we should believe anything Skinner says if everything he thinks and does is predetermined? But if this is what he believes, and it is what many people believe today, what makes anyone or anything special? For if we are all just 'dancing to our DNA', then that makes DNA special, but it makes us puppets. Somehow, the part has become more special than the whole. We are not the main characters in the story any more, our DNA is.

Am I special?

No surprise then, that many young people are growing up today wondering to themselves: 'Am I even special? Am I even significant?'

Is there anything which makes a human being special or significant?

Jean-Paul Sartre was perhaps the most famous philosopher of the twentieth century. As an atheist, he argued that there is nothing that makes us essentially human, let alone essentially special. He reasoned that, since there is no God who has designed us, a human has no blueprint, no essence, no nature. Therefore, we must create our own nature, value and identity. It was Sartre's partner, Simone de Beauvoir, who – from the same existentialist perspective – observed that one is not born a man or a woman, one becomes one. You lead your nature where you want it to go because it does not offer you a script, a plan or a path. You can be a man, a woman or a mix. You can pursue sexual relationships with the same sex, the opposite sex or a mix. In short, you can do whatever you want. You are free to make yourself and remake yourself ad infinitum because you aren't defined and don't have to be defined by anything except your own desires.

But here's the question. If, in Sartre's view, a human being comes into the world with no innate identity, why do we feel the need to create an identity? Where does that longing, for an identity that we apparently do not have, come from? A dog has no such problems being no one special. Provided it is watered, fed, housed and patted, a dog is content. Dogs don't worry themselves with existential concerns. Why do we? Why do we even care whether or not our life is significant?

Well, I want to suggest that the reason we have a fundamental human need to be significant is because we *are* significant. We want to be special because we are! Even our fairy stories tell us this. The Ugly Duckling, Cinderella, Shrek 1, 2 and 3 – all speak of the human longing to be somebody special.

But sadly, we don't often feel that significant or special.

I spent the majority of my school years stifled by a constant sense of self-consciousness and an anxiety that – actually, if I was honest with myself – I really wasn't that significant, I really wasn't standing out from the crowd, I really wasn't anybody special. I remember I worked in a supermarket after school and weekends pushing trolleys and stacking shelves for the princely sum of about £4 an hour. Just saving a couple of hundred pounds took weeks of work but for some reason, I decided that it made sense for me to spend £200 of my hard-earned cash to buy a pair of really cool sunglasses, on the basis that this would greatly enhance my coolness factor. Now, they were cool sunglasses – Oakley Razor Sunglasses, the sort of rainbow-tinted, wraparound sunglasses that a lot of the Australian cricketers were wearing at the time.

I believed, exactly as the clever advertisers wanted me to believe – that if significant people, like these sporting greats, were wearing these glasses, then if I wore them, that would mean (by a process of indisputable logic) that I, too, would be significant. I would become cool. I would be a somebody.

23

Can you relate to what I'm talking about here or am I the only one who has experienced anxiety about whether or not I'm important? Whether or not other people look at me and think, 'Now there's somebody special'? Or whether, when they look at me, they just keep on looking right through me?

It is often said that we shouldn't worry about what other people are thinking about us – because they are not, they are thinking about themselves. This is so true. I wish someone older and wiser had pointed that simple truth out to me back when I was a young man. But it's easy to fall into anxiety about how others rate us on the social scale of significance. There is even a name for this type of anxiety. It's called status anxiety. The philosopher Alain de Botton, in describing status anxiety, explains that people who hold important positions in society are commonly labelled 'somebodies', and everyone else we label 'nobodies'. 'Somebodies' are highly visible and admired. 'Nobodies' are all but invisible.

One of our greatest fears as human beings is to be unseen, to be invisible. Nobody wants to be invisible. Nobody wants to be a nobody. But in a world of seven billion people, not everybody, we reason, can be a somebody.

So, where does that leave us? It leaves us in competition . . . with everybody!

Life as a competition

Everybody is competing with everybody to be a somebody. To be significant. To stand out from the nameless faces in the crowd.

But wouldn't you agree that everybody in competition with everybody is not the healthiest foundation for universal human happiness and flourishing? Sadly however, competition is the narrative by which we increasingly live.

Have you ever noticed how many movies and TV shows depict life as a competition and other human beings as the competition?

Think of Katniss Everdeen in *The Hunger Games*, Frank Underwood in *House of Cards* or Daenerys Targaryen in *Game of Thrones*. For many people, these shows are accurate and insightful metaphors, revealing life for what it really is – a game with winners and losers. And as these shows make graphically clear, it really doesn't pay to be a loser in the game of life.

Unsurprisingly, so many today are growing up with the view that unless they make it to the top, they will never be significant, and they will never be happy. And getting to the top normally means becoming wealthy, famous or the best in one's field of study, sport, career or art. And unless we become wealthy, famous or the best in our field, we have failed at life, we have failed as a person. We are a failure.

But I want to tell you: that is the wrong narrative to live by.

If you have ever been told that you are a failure or told yourself that you are, it is not true. It's a lie. Because failure is an event, it is not a person. To equate failing with *being* a failure is to make the mistake of conflating what you do with who you are. But they are not the same thing.

Second, according to research by the University of Michigan's Institute for Social Research, trying to base one's sense of self-worth and significance on *external* sources of achievement, such as physical appearance or success in career, study, sport, music, travel or relationships, results in more stress, anger, academic problems, relationship conflicts and higher levels of drug and alcohol use as well as symptoms of eating disorders. Why is that? Well, let me suggest some possible reasons.

Those who measure their significance as a person in terms of accomplishment, or success, or in what they are able to do or achieve, often find that their focus in life is always on the pursuit of the next goal, whatever it may be – wealth, family, career, relationship. These goals and their attainment come to define the person's sense of self entirely, so that over time, his or her life's motto subconsciously becomes: 'I achieve, therefore I am.' In other words, I am what I do. Does that feel uncomfortably familiar?

Now, among the many problems associated with this mindset or approach to life is that, if I think that I am what I do, then my personal sense of significance will be judged on how well I feel I am doing; but how well I feel I am doing will inevitably be based on how well I feel I am doing in comparison to others. But if that is the case, then I am now in a position where my sense of significance has actually become inversely proportional to how well others around me are doing. And if that's the case it becomes difficult to celebrate the success of others in a genuine way.

In other words, basing our sense of significance entirely on what we do and what we achieve will ultimately have negative effects on the way we see ourselves and the way we see each other.

I mentioned that I worked in a supermarket in my youth. And if you have ever worked in retail, you will know that a product's success has much to do with where it is placed on the shelf. According to the research, shoppers start looking at the shelf at eye level, work from left to right, and make their purchasing decision in fewer than eight seconds. If your product isn't one that people are choosing in that eight-second window, then retailers aren't going to continue to let that product take up valuable shelf space.

And that's why eye-catching packaging and clever marketing of products are hugely important. The different suppliers, who come into the shop, try all sorts of ways to convince the shop's owner to put their particular product in the places on the shelves that attract the most buyers, which is usually eye level because 'eye level is buy level'. So, the motivated suppliers will try to persuade the shop's owner and offer a variety of incentives to get the owner to do this.

And it is really interesting when two competing suppliers are in the shop at the same time. Rarely do they smile at each other and say: 'Isn't it cool that we sell really similar products?' Usually, they don't even acknowledge the other person or do so in an awkward way.

Think then, what happens to human relationships when everybody is competing with everybody for that contested shelf space? That coveted space where we are seen, recognized, valued and chosen by others?

What happens is that we tend to treat ourselves and others as objects, comparing and evaluating one another in the way we value products in the marketplace. For years, sociologists have been talking about the increasing objectification of human beings. You see it in the world of sport, where players are traded between teams like commodities on a stock market, or in business where employees can be poached from other companies or simply let go and replaced with newer, better models. The same happens on university campuses where students sometimes face the prospect of being literally bid on, auction style, in a very public process of determining who makes it into the most popular sororities and fraternities on Ivy-league campuses and who doesn't.

But this general trend towards objectification or commodification of the human person has received a huge turbo-boost in recent years through the way in which social media technology is shaping society.

Social media and self

In the critically acclaimed sci-fi series *Black Mirror*, each episode explores in disturbing detail the ways in which technology is shaping our society. One of the most memorable episodes imagines a world in the not-too-distant future in which we are completely dependent upon social media and people can rate one another, out of 5 stars, based on appearance and even the briefest of interactions, everything from the way you looked at the person travelling opposite you on the tube, to the lack of enthusiasm you displayed for the birthday gift your co-worker gave you. And these ratings have real-world implications: drop below 4 stars and you will start to lose some friends, or plummet below 3 stars and you could lose your job or be barred from certain businesses or gatherings. As one article in *Business Insider* magazine puts it:

> It's actually not too far-fetched from the world we live in now. Just imagine if you combined your Uber rating with the amount of likes you got on Facebook and the number of replies you received on Twitter in the last month. Now imagine that that singular rating determined everything about your life, from where you worked to the home you were eligible to live in.

This episode got a lot of people talking, wondering whether this was just a parody of the way things are now, or whether it was a prophetic vision of where we are headed if we are not careful.

A recent report in the UK entitled #StatusofMind, on how social media platforms are having an impact on the well-being of young people today has concluded that Instagram, Snapchat, Facebook and Twitter all demonstrated decidedly negative effects on young people's overall mental health, increasing users' anxiety, depression, and problems with self-identity and body image. The author of the report, Matt Keracher, said these platforms draw young people to 'compare themselves against unrealistic, largely curated, filtered and Photoshopped versions of reality'.

Journalists are commenting on the increasingly desperate attempts teenage girls in particular are going to in order to make their profile pictures sexier and more alluring and therefore more likely to get the likes they want – an important definition of success.

According to Dr Jessica Strubel, who presented an important study to the American Psychological Association on the effect of new dating apps of the likes of Tinder: 'People are living in a surreal world, creating these unattainable ideals and expectations that no one can meet. It's creating a 24/7 constant need for impression and appearance management.'

The UK's National Health Service (NHS) has reported that the numbers of young people being admitted to hospital suffering from anxiety has tripled in just the last five years, and John Cameron, who heads the leading national helpline for young people, in a recent article in *The Telegraph*, said: 'These problems are often impacted by a need to keep up with friends and to have the perfect life; and the 24/7 nature of technology means that young people can never escape this pressure.'

I've heard it said that the family home might be one of the few places in the world where young people can learn that they are loved not because of what they do, but because of who they are. They certainly won't learn it on Instagram or in the world of online dating, or the classroom, or the workplace. Sadly, parents, in their love and desire to see their children succeed in what they know is a competitive society, sometimes inadvertently communicate a message to their children that sounds not dissimilar to the message they are already receiving from the world: 'Perform and we might see you, achieve and we might love you.'

My daughter, Grace, often sings out loud to herself when she is alone and thinks that no one can hear her. As a father, I was so happy when I overheard Grace, then four years old, singing these words to herself in her bedroom: 'Daddy loves me, he really loves me, even if I'm really, really bad, he still loves me, and Jesus will always love me too!'

I thought to myself: 'Yes! She gets it!' Her heart has received it. That she's loved for who she is, not for how she behaves or what she achieves.

But it's not just kids, or young adults, who struggle to realize their innate value and worth. For this is part of the problem of the human story: we are all trying to find significance and self-worth in what we do, what we can obtain and achieve – and it's not working.

It's not working

It's not working because we are living weighed down by a responsibility that we were never designed to bear. The constant and relentless burden of trying to prove or establish our sense of self, our name, our reputation in the world.

The freedom that Sartre, de Beauvoir and other existentialist philosophers talked about – the freedom to make yourself and remake yourself ad infinitum because you aren't defined by anything except your own desires – is not a freedom, it's a slavery. Because it's all on you. The relentless task of having to create or manufacture your own sense of identity, self-worth and significance. It's all on you, and if you were born after 1980 and live on social media, it's a 24/7, full-time job. And there's no guarantee that even if you work at it really hard, the world around you is going to say: 'Hey, now there's a somebody worth looking at!'

In fact, even the small percentage of people who do achieve the sort of wealth, fame, popularity and success that make a person stand out from the crowd is not necessarily finding that with that success really come the happiness and fulfilment they thought it would bring. Here are some examples.

Perhaps one of the biggest somebodies of the twentieth century, arguably the biggest celebrity of the modern era, was the King, Mr Elvis Presley. A reporter once asked Presley the following question: 'Elvis, when you first started playing music, you said you wanted to be rich, famous and happy. You're now rich and famous. Are you happy?' To which Elvis replied: 'I am lonely as hell'. And that was six weeks before he died.

Markus Persson is a legend in the world of gaming – the creator of Minecraft, perhaps the most popular and successful computer game in history. He sold it to Microsoft for 2.5 billion US dollars. Months later, he wrote the following tweet, 'hanging out in Ibiza with a bunch of friends and partying with famous people, able to do whatever I wanted, and I've never felt more isolated'.

The actor Nicole Kidman said it was winning an Oscar in 2002 that made her realize how empty her life really was.

Few things in life, it seems, are more isolating and depressing than to experience that which you thought would bring the ultimate feeling of self-worth and significance, and it has failed to deliver.

A matter of soul

Interestingly, when measured on the scales of global celebrity and world influence, Jesus is probably the most significant person who has ever lived. During his life on this earth he often spoke before vast crowds of people, but he never drew his sense of significance from those crowds. He knew that one day, they could be worshipping him and another day trying to kill him. Such is the fickleness of the crowd.

Speaking once to a crowd of people, Jesus asked them the following penetrating question: 'What good is it if someone gains the whole world but loses their soul?' (Matthew 16.26, NIrV).

According to Jesus, it is actually possible to gain everything in life which you thought would make you special and, in the process, lose the only thing in life which really does make you special – your soul.

From the perspective of Christianity, the most important thing about you is not anything that can be seen from the outside. The most important thing about you is your soul – for your soul is the life centre of you. And, says Jesus, your soul is more valuable than anything else in the whole world. For, it is the only soul you will ever have, and it is made for eternity. It is made for God. Like a precious Stradivarius violin, your soul bears the image of its

Maker, and however invisible you may sometimes feel, you are not invisible to your Maker, for you are – the Bible says – the apple of God's eye. Neither a mistake, nor an accident, nor a failure. As Christian philosopher Dallas Willard puts it: 'You're an unceasing spiritual being, purposely made, for an eternal future in God's great universe.'

If this is true, it would explain why superficial and transitory things like money, or fame and success, though perfectly fine things in themselves, do not and cannot ultimately fulfil us. For they are incapable of offering that which our *souls* most deeply crave, which is to be fully seen, known and loved, everlastingly.

The Bible claims that such love as this can only be found in God, and that it's because we have lost our connection to the love of God that our souls are sick. It calls this sickness 'sin' and asserts it is this soul-sickness that causes us to compete rather than cooperate, to objectify rather than dignify, to denigrate rather than celebrate, to pull others down rather than lift them up, and to envy and resent rather than love and respect.

When it comes to recording the lives of Jesus' early followers, the Bible doesn't whitewash or gloss over their foibles and failings. And, if there's anyone in the Bible who you might think typifies the person who has swallowed the big lie that one must achieve something in order to become somebody special, it was a man called Saul of Tarsus. As the Bible explains, Saul was a child of the best upbringing, a student of the renowned teacher Gamaliel, educated in elite Jewish schools. He was on the path to success, being prepared, perhaps, to become Chief Priest, even. Before he encountered Jesus, he thought of himself as a moral man, yet he had been willing to do anything in order to get ahead in his career as a religious leader, including destroying the lives of others. He even persecuted the early followers of Jesus of Nazareth for challenging the religious establishment. He rounded up families, sent them to prison and even condoned the killing of a follower of Jesus named

Stephen. He thought of himself as called by God, but he wasn't called, he was just driven. He felt as if he was called to make a name for God, when really, he was just trying to make a name for himself.

Saul was zealous, religious even, but he hadn't yet encountered the love of God. But when he did, everything changed. In a dramatic moment of encounter, the Bible records that Jesus met Paul on the road to Damascus, and to cut a long story short, the Lord Jesus relieved Saul of the burden of having to manufacture a name for himself. In Jesus, Saul discovered God's love, as well as an identity and a calling that no earthy honour, award or prestige could ever beat. And this proud, driven, graceless, religious moralist known as Saul – who had wanted to be so big and successful – changed his name to Paul, which means 'small' or 'humble'. He came, in fact, to be known as the apostle Paul, servant to all people, both Jews and Gentiles. Before he met Jesus, he thought he saw life as it really was – a competition to be won – but Jesus helped him see life as it is really meant to be. No wonder, in one of his letters to the church in Corinth, Paul penned one of the most moving pieces of writing on love ever written:

> If I speak in the tongues of men or of angels, but do not have love, I am only a resounding gong or a clanging cymbal. If I have the gift of prophecy and can fathom all mysteries and all knowledge, and if I have a faith that can move mountains, but do not have love, I am nothing. If I give all I possess to the poor and give over my body to hardship that I may boast, but do not have love, I gain nothing.
>
> Love is patient, love is kind. It does not envy, it does not boast, it is not proud. It does not dishonour others, it is not self-seeking, it is not easily angered, it keeps no record of wrongs.
> (1 Corinthians 13.1–4, NIV)

Jesus helped Paul realize that life is not a competition to be won, it is a privilege and an opportunity to love and to be loved. The purpose of your life, according to Jesus, is to love, and to be loved. This is what life is all about. This is the real music that our souls were created to play. To love and to be loved. And, says Jesus, it all starts with receiving the love of God.

The Christian claim is that when you taste this love, you realize you do not need to make a name for yourself in order to become someone special because you already are special. You come to understand that you are already *seen*, *recognized*, *valued* and *chosen* by your Maker and that this is more precious than anything this world has to offer: to know, in the depths of your soul, that you are loved by God; created in his image; and that the question of 'who you are', is finally answered in the reality of 'whose you are' – God's. You are a child of the Creator of the universe, and you bear on your soul his signature. The signature of the master craftsman.

3

The matter of goodness

Why do the right thing when it's not the easy thing?

Who am I?

Quick quiz question. Who am I? I was born in 1971 in the United States. At age 16, I began competing in triathlons and became national sprint course champion in 1989 and 1990. In 1992, I began my career as a professional cyclist. I won the World Championship in 1993. Three years later, I was diagnosed with cancer. I recovered and returned to cycling in 1998. I won the Tour de France that year and for the next seven years in a row, from 1998 to 2005.

I am (you've probably guessed it by now) . . . Lance Armstrong.

We love winners. Particularly those who overcome adversity. But why is Lance Armstrong, one of the biggest winners and overcomers of all time, not loved by many people today? Because he cheated. He did the wrong thing. He took performance enhancing drugs.

We love winners, but it seems that, as human beings, we don't like cheaters. We don't admire people who do the wrong thing. Why is that?

I mean, animals don't seem to care about questions of ethics or morality. When a wolf opportunistically attacks the youngest, weakest deer in the pack, the other wolves don't accuse him of bad sportsmanship. And when a cat torments a mouse just for fun, the other cats do not tell him to pick on someone his own size.

Humans are clearly different from other animals in this respect. For animals, it's the law of the jungle. For us, we are also aware of another law: a *moral* law. For instance, what do we call someone who acts without regard to a moral law? An animal! And it's not a term of endearment.

Doing the right thing

As human beings, we don't just look at the world through the lens of what is. We also judge the world through the lens of what ought to be. We cannot help but think like that – that some things are right and others wrong.

And so, it makes us angry when we hear about cheating and corruption in sport – think, for example, of match-fixing scandals in cricket or baseball. Or in business – think of the emissions scandal of the Volkswagen company, which tried to trick the environmental agency about the amount of pollution its cars were emitting into the atmosphere. Or in politics – think of ministers' expense scandals or 'cash-for-access-to-politicians' scandals.

When we think of examples like these, we probably think: 'Wouldn't it be great if we could somehow end cheating, corruption and unethical behaviour in society all together? Wouldn't the world be a better place?'

Well, here's an interesting question: why don't we end these things? If we don't like cheating, corruption and unethical behaviour, why not get rid of them?

The problem, as it turns out, is that it's just not that easy. As Dallas Willard puts it: 'The human condition is one where we don't want to do what is bad, but we find it necessary.' Have you ever noticed that? How doing the right thing, like telling the truth for example, sometimes seems to be in conflict with our comfort or happiness?

Once, in a Sunday school class, a little girl was asked: 'What is a lie?' And she said: 'It is an abomination to God, and a very present help in times of trouble!'

Doing the right thing is not always the easy thing to do.

We all do it

Let us consider the problem of cheating. Whether in sport, business or politics, we tend to assume that cheating is done by just a few bad apples, and if we got rid of those bad apples, then most of the lying, cheating and unethical behaviour that takes place in the world would be dealt with.

But unfortunately, all the research shows that's not the case. In his book, *The (Honest) Truth about Dishonesty*, Dan Ariely, Professor of psychology and behavioural economics at Duke University, explains that most of the cheating that takes place in society is actually made up of different and subtle kinds of dishonest acts that we all practise on a regular basis, and together these acts have a big cumulative effect.

He cites several case studies to illustrate this. For example, in one case study, he talks about the mystery surrounding a gift shop in Washington DC's Arts Centre which was found to be losing $150,000 a year. As payments were made into a cash box, rather than a register, the first assumption was that someone was stealing.

However, after firing the person they thought was responsible, the losses continued until they eventually discovered that the problem was not just one thief, but many well-meaning volunteers each 'borrowing' small amounts of money over the course of the year but somehow never getting around to returning that money.

According to Professor Ariely, all the case studies show that the problem of cheating and unethical behaviour in society is not one of just a few bad apples or rogue operators spoiling it for everyone else. The bad news, says Ariely, is that we all take moral shortcuts. We all cheat.

We *all* cheat!

Ariely explains that the heart of the issue is that humans live with two opposing fundamental motivations: on the one hand, we

37

want to see ourselves as good, honest and upright people, we really do; but on the other hand, we desire to gain the benefits that could come from cheating. In other words, we want to be able to look at ourselves in the mirror each day and see a good person staring back at us, but we are also prepared to do whatever will help us get ahead in life.

So, how do we handle these conflicting desires? We do so, Ariely says, through a process of rationalization – in essence, we lie to ourselves. We see this dynamic at work, for example, in a case study undertaken by psychologists that involved placing a six-pack of coke and several one-dollar bills into a fridge used by students. The students knew that the money and drinks belonged to someone else and were off-limits. What do you think happened? While the money remained untouched in the refrigerator, every can of coke was eventually taken.

Why? Because we all know that we shouldn't steal, and taking cash would be blatantly stealing – doing what our conscience tells us we shouldn't do. However, the students were able to take a can of coke and rationalize in their minds that it wasn't *really* stealing, even though those cans were of course purchased with money.

Professor Ariely calls this ability to deceive ourselves *cognitive flexibility*. It allows us to get what we want through cheating but still think of ourselves as good people.

The other thing about cheating and dishonesty is, that the more socially acceptable cheating appears to be, the more likely we are to give in to it. For example, in another case study, psychologists had participants take a maths test, in which they would be rewarded one dollar for every correct answer. But they could also mark their own paper, giving participants the opportunity to cheat. And of course, lots of people did cheat. But in one room, an actor was secretly added to the experiment and pretended to get 100 per cent of the answers right within an impossibly short time and was rewarded for it in front of everyone. By witnessing a single person blatantly getting away with cheating, participants in this class cheated twice as much as in other classes. Showing, as did many other experiments, that we human beings are incredibly vulnerable to the group environment.

Once cheating or other unethical behaviour starts, says Professor Ariely, it tends to gain momentum and becomes contagious. Which is why he suggests that businesses shouldn't tolerate even small indiscretions; because it lowers the bar for everyone.

In short, his research highlights just how morally fallible we all are, even those of us with good intentions, which is actually most of us.

So then, how do we solve the problem of unethical behaviour if virtually everyone is the problem? How do we, for example, solve the problem of cheating if, as the research shows, virtually everyone does it in one way or the other?

It seems to me that if we are successfully going to tackle the problem of unethical behaviour in society, such as lying and cheating, which we've identified is more subtle, contagious and widespread than most people are aware, we need to think carefully about the question of 'why?'.

Why be good? Why do the right thing? Why not cheat?

Why be good?

The usual answer given is that if everyone cheats, we will all be worse off. For example, in business, the answer to the question, 'Why not cheat?', is that it won't be profitable for the businesses (because they will lose people's trust), and it won't be profitable for the employees (because they may be fired or demoted).

But what if I discover, as an individual within a company, that acting unethically would actually be better for me personally, even if not for the company? What if my personal bank account would be better off if I cheated a bit, or what if my personal career trajectory would improve if I lied a little bit? And what if I knew I wouldn't get caught? What then is my motivation to act ethically?

Or if you are a student, what if you really could get a better grade on your essay by cheating and you knew you wouldn't get caught? What reason would you have then to do the right thing?

These are questions that get right to the heart of everything, yet surprisingly, ethics courses rarely seem to address them, even though they are perhaps the most fundamental or basic questions in morality. Why not cheat if you can get away with it and end up with everything you want?

The ancient Greek philosopher, Plato, deals with this question in his famous work, *The Republic*. In it, we find a very interesting dialogue between Plato's teacher Socrates and a man by the name of Thrasymachus. Thrasymachus is what we might call a radical moral sceptic. That means, like many people today, Thrasymachus believes there is no objective moral law. So he says to Socrates something like, 'Look, don't be naive, there are no moral absolutes. The end justifies the means; justice is just a mask for power; and ethics is just a bunch of rules that other people invent, it's not a real thing, so there's no reason why we shouldn't cheat if cheating helps us to win. No reason why we shouldn't lie if lying helps us avoid pain. No reason why we shouldn't be unethical if being unethical helps us to get what we want.'

He then illustrates his point by referring to the ancient Greek myth of Gyges, a poor and lowly shepherd who hates being a nobody. One day, Gyges the shepherd discovers a magic ring that gives him the power to be invisible. He realizes the ring can help him to become a successful *somebody* because with it, he can do whatever he wants and get away with it. So, what does Gyges do with this ring of power? He uses it to kill the king, marry the queen and eventually rule the kingdom – and, all the while, fool everyone into believing that he is a really great person.

Therefore, the question Thrasymachus asks Socrates is: why not be unethical – if, like Gyges the shepherd, you know you can get away with it and receive everything you ever wanted?

It's a very difficult question to answer if (like Thrasymachus) you don't believe in an objective moral law because you might think: 'Who wouldn't want to have everything they've ever thought would make them happy?' And if you believe that ethics is just a bunch of rules that other people have invented, then why should you let those rules put any limits on your happiness?

Responding to the challenge

In light of Thrasymachus' challenging question, it seems to me that if we really hope to find a cure or solution to the problem of unethical behaviour in society – which we've established is not just down to a few bad apples, but to all of us – at least three things are needed:

1 a good reason to be good
2 help to be good
3 grace when we fall.

Interestingly, the Christian claim is that all three of these things uniquely converge in the person of Jesus Christ. Let's look at each of these claims in turn.

A good reason to be good

When ethics is taught today, most of the teaching is about how to be ethical, but not why. Sometimes the most fundamental question is not even addressed, which is: where do the moral values to which we all aspire – such as justice, generosity or courage – actually come from? This might sound like a merely abstract question, but it's really a highly practical one.

Let me try to illustrate the practicality of the issue with an example. As an Australian, I have observed that one of the biggest moral issues facing people in Britain today is whether, when eating a scone, one should first spread on the cream, followed by the jam on top, or whether one should first apply the jam, followed by the cream on top. As an innocent stranger from a foreign country, I've discovered that people in Britain can get very worked up about this. Each scone-eating camp believes that the other is clearly wrong.

Now, that was a humorous example, but here's a serious issue. If I were to ask you if racism is wrong, my guess is that you would say it is. I rarely meet anyone who believes otherwise. But when we say racism is wrong, what do we mean by saying, 'it's wrong'? Do we mean it is wrong in the same way that the equation $2 + 2 = 5$ is wrong? Or do we mean it is wrong in the same way that jam first on a scone and then cream is wrong?

Now, from where I sit as a Christian, when I say racism is wrong, I mean that it is wrong in the same way I mean $2 + 2 = 5$ is wrong. I mean it is wrong in fact. Why? Because, from my point of view, just as there are mathematical laws that we did not create as human beings, so too, there are moral laws we did not create as human beings. They exist independently of us. Outside of us.

If, however, I am, say, a secular humanist – someone who doesn't believe in God but does believe in good moral values such as justice and equality – I might believe that we don't discover morality, we create it. We choose it. In other words, we decide for ourselves if racism is wrong.

Yet, if that's the case, what if other people decide for themselves that racism is *not* wrong? What if they decide for themselves that racism is actually good? If I am a secular humanist, on what basis can I tell them that they are wrong?

I cannot appeal to reason. Reason cannot decide here, for there is no syllogism or logical formula that proves racism is right or wrong. Nor can I appeal to science. Science cannot decide here either, for there is no scientific experiment that proves racism is right or wrong. If I am a secular humanist, it seems that I have no ground to stand on other than my preference for equality, just as racists have no ground to stand on other than their own preference for racism.

And this is where secular humanism contradicts itself, for on the one hand, it says that Mr Smith must decide for himself what is good, but on the other hand, it wishes to say that Mr Smith ought to respect all people. But if Mr Smith says: 'Well, I have decided for myself that people with skin of a different colour from mine are not to be respected', what can secular humanists say in response? They might want to say to Mr Smith: 'You've made the wrong decision because we ought to respect all people regardless of skin colour.' But they can't do that if they believe that people have to decide for themselves what is good.

So, secular humanism finds itself conflicted. It offers us a case for good moral values (such as justice, equality and respect for human freedom) but without providing a rational foundation or philosophical soil within which to root such values.

C. S. Lewis argues that for ethics to be effective, it needs to operate on three levels, which he illustrates using a metaphor of a group of ships out at sea. Level one is about making sure that the ships don't bump into each other – he says this is like social ethics, which are rules about how to get along with each other. Level two is about making sure the individual ships are seaworthy – that is, capable of steering and staying afloat. This, he compares to personal ethics, which are ethics relating to character and virtue. However, level three, he explains, is about the most fundamental question of all: why are the boats in the water in the first place? What's their mission? What's their purpose?

This is the most fundamental of questions, not just for every society, institution or fleet of ships out at sea, but for every individual person as well. What's my purpose? Why am I here on this planet in the first place?

We need to get that fundamental question right for everything else to be right. For example, if we assume – as Socrates did – that getting rich is not the *main* purpose of human life (because money is meant to be a means, not an end), but you decide nevertheless that your *main* purpose in life is to become wealthy, then Socrates would say it makes little moral difference if you become wealthy by lying and cheating or by honest diligence and hard work. Why? Because in the first instance, you are being bad for a bad reason, and in the second instance, you are being good for a bad reason. But living the good life (says Socrates) is about being good for a good reason. It is about living in alignment with your purpose.

However, if you believe, as many do today, that we are all here as the result of a random combination of time plus matter plus chance, it makes it really rather difficult to point to any ultimate purpose in life, and therefore to any solid foundation for the ethical standards that we are trying so hard to uphold.

Immanuel Kant once observed that in order for the moral choice to be the rational choice, we must believe that living morally will eventually lead to our happiness. Because nobody wants to be unhappy, in the end. But as Kant also recognized, if there is no God and the universe is nothing more than a blind mechanical system, there is no guarantee that morality will end in happiness, nor is it certain that cheaters will never prosper.

The remarkable claim of Christianity, however, is that there is more to this life than unguided laws operating on mindless atoms. The claim is that you and I are here not *by accident*, at all, but here *on purpose* because somebody, God, wanted us to be here. If this is true, then there are at least two profound implications that flow from this truth. First, it means that there is an answer to the question: 'Why am I here on this planet in the first place?' And that means that there is an ultimate purpose in life and

44

therefore a solid and objective foundation for morality – for good and for evil: goodness being that which is in alignment with our purpose, and evil being that which violates it. As we have already seen, according to Christianity, the primary purpose of our lives is to love and to be loved, and it all starts with receiving the love of God.

Second, it means that when we live in accordance with our purpose (that is, when we love rather than hate, heal rather than hurt, and lift others up rather than tear them down) and when we do what we know is right, even when it's not easy, then we flourish as human beings, both inside and out – because we are living the life that we were made to live. Conversely, it also means that when we live in violation of our purpose – that is, when we lie or cheat or take moral shortcuts in order to achieve that which we think will make us happy – it actually won't make us happy in the end, even if we never get caught.

In other words, it means that doing the right thing, even when it's not easy, ultimately is worth it.

Help to be good

Having a good reason to be good, however, though essential, is not sufficient because, as we have seen, we are all susceptible to the temptations of cheating or of taking a moral shortcut, even when we have the best of intentions. We also need help to be good.

In his thirties, sometime around the year 1870, Andrew Carnegie, who later in life became one of the wealthiest men of the twentieth century, tried to maintain his integrity by vowing to give up business, so that he would not get caught up in 'the debasing idolatry of amassing power and wealth'. Yet, when the time of his economic success came, he was unwilling to leave the path of 'making money at any cost', and unfortunately, some of the character-degrading effects he had feared at a young age eventually manifested themselves in his later life. Even though he became a great philanthropist who built thousands of libraries, his employees said they would have much preferred if he had just offered them humane working conditions. It has been stated that the working conditions, and in particular, long hours that Carnegie demanded from his factory workers in the pursuit of profit, were so harsh, and the housing situation so deplorable, that many of his employees died from accidents or disease in their forties or even earlier.

As Jesus said: 'What good is it if someone gains the whole world but loses their soul?' (Matthew 16.26, nirv).

To be fair, most people don't wilfully sell their souls to the 'ring of power' like Gyges the shepherd or Gollum in the *Lord of the Rings*, whose character was inspired by the myth of Gyges – abandoning all moral conscience in the unbridled pursuit of power, pleasure or success. Most of us don't intentionally leap off an ethical cliff into some sort of morally relativistic free fall. Most of us are actually trying to do the right thing most of the time. We find ourselves falling, but if we fall, it is not because we embraced amorality, but because we find ourselves slipping downhill, morally, bit by bit, despite our best efforts – that is, we do not tend to fall, morally, like Gollum, but more like Frodo. You see, Frodo was a good hobbit, but over time, the ring slowly got a hold of him – fatigue, tiredness, the pressures of responsibility, the suggestive whispers of Gollum and the gradual weakening of the will all conspired until eventually, as some of you may remember, Frodo fails. At the critical moment, he falls, morally; he can't give up the ring of power and gives himself over to it; he throws the good aside. And in the end, it is only an unlikely act of divine providence that saves him and everyone else.

How do we fight unethical behaviour and corruption in society if we can't even win the battle for goodness in our own lives? How do we deal with the problem out there if we are also dealing with the problem inside of us? That's the real challenge we face. If the heart of the human problem is the problem of the human heart, how do we heal ourselves? How do we get out of this pattern of rationalization and self-deception?

It is interesting that although it was written centuries before modern psychology, the Bible speaks about this inner conflict of desires in the human psyche (psyche is the Greek word for soul). Remember Saul of Tarsus, who became the apostle Paul? He had thought of himself as a moral man, but at the same time, he was willing to do almost anything in order to get ahead, including destroying the lives of others. In one of his letters to the early Church, which you can find in the Bible, there is a very honest account of his struggles with goodness, with doing the right thing, even when it is not the easy thing to do. He writes:

> I don't understand myself at all, for I really want to do what is right, but I can't. I do what I don't want to – what I hate. I know perfectly well that what I am doing is wrong, and my bad conscience proves that I agree with these laws I am breaking. But I can't help myself . . . No matter which way I turn I can't make myself do right. I want to but I can't. When I want to do good, I don't, and when I try not to do wrong. I do it anyway. (Romans 7.15–16, 18–19, TLB)

Which of us cannot sympathize, in one way or another, with this battle for goodness that we don't always win? But Paul's letter is not all negative. He goes on to say that in Jesus he found help with this battle, describing this help as a liberation from slavery – in this case, the slavery of doing what we know is wrong, over and over again. A sort of slavery to self. Asking rhetorically in his letter, who will free him from this slavery, Paul concludes with a note of rejoicing: 'Thank God! It has been done by Jesus Christ our Lord. He has set me free' (Romans 7.25, TLB).

That was Paul's personal experience that he wanted to share with others: that in the person of Jesus Christ he had genuinely found a new source of moral and spiritual power in his life. Alone, he says, he had been unable to free himself from patterns of behaviour that put him at odds with his own conscience. Yet, he says, when he encountered Jesus, he found a way out – a sense of freedom. Not the freedom to live however he wanted, but the freedom to live as he ought. The freedom to choose the good.

Grace when we fall

There's an old story about two pastors who were going to visit a man whose wife had left him after she caught him cheating on her. As they were on their way to counsel him, the older pastor asked the younger one, 'Do you think you could ever do something like that?', to which the younger pastor responded, 'No, there's no way I could ever do something despicable like that.' The older pastor replied: 'Well, you better go home then. I will take care of this one alone.'

Human experience, as well as modern psychology, shows us that we are so morally fallible as human beings. Even those of us with the best intentions can fall. And the less we realize this, the more susceptible we are.

We see this dynamic at work in the lives of the many revered men and women recorded in the Bible. All the well-known characters – Adam, Eve, Abraham, Sarah, Moses, Miriam, David, Peter, Paul, just to name a few – they all fail, morally. And often in big ways.

I think that's surprising to a lot of people unfamiliar with Christianity. There is a perception that Christianity is all about being a good person, like a club for people who think that they are holier than everyone else. But according to the Bible, being a Christian is not primarily about being a good person, it is about being in a relationship with a person (God) who is good. Perfectly good. But this perfectly good God does not say to us: 'You also must be perfectly good, or else.' The Christian story is that through Jesus all are invited – as good or as bad as they are – into relationship with him.

Christians call this message (that we don't have to be good enough to be accepted by God) 'good news', and the word they use to describe God's dealing with us in this way is '*grace*'. Grace means getting what you don't deserve, in a good way.

We see this grace, for example, in a story recorded in the Bible about an encounter between Jesus and a man named Zacchaeus. Interestingly, the name Zacchaeus means 'righteous'. It indicates to us that Zacchaeus probably came from a religious family. But as it turns out, his name must have sounded like a joke to those who knew him because Zacchaeus was anything but righteous. Rather than growing up to be a good Jewish boy, as his parents might have hoped, Zacchaeus had chosen to be part of the great political system that was, at that point in history, oppressing the Jewish people: he had become a tax collector for the Roman Empire. A chief tax collector no less. Collecting money from his own Jewish people to give to the Roman overlords, while at the same time taking a slice of that money for himself.

No surprise, then, that although Zacchaeus was a wealthy man, he was generally despised for his unethical and self-seeking behaviour.

Yet, the Bible story takes an unexpected turn. Maybe it was because he was simply curious or perhaps, he genuinely felt that something important was missing from his life – either way, something about Jesus captured Zacchaeus' attention. So much so that, as the Bible recounts, he went to extraordinary lengths to catch a glimpse of Jesus when he passed through Jericho. Being a short man, he was not able to see over the gathered crowds that usually accompanied Jesus' arrival into a village. So, Zacchaeus unceremoniously climbed up a sycamore tree to get a good view of Jesus as he passed by. When Jesus eventually came across the place where Zacchaeus was, he stopped, looked up and saw Zacchaeus; and, in a dramatic moment of encounter, he called Zacchaeus by name and told him to come down immediately so that he could visit his house.

To the moralists and religious legalists of Jesus' time, this would have been outrageous. Zacchaeus was a cheat, a swindler, a traitor to his own people. He was a moral failure. Jesus should not have spoken to him, let alone invited himself to Zacchaeus' house. Zacchaeus deserved nothing but rejection and alienation.

Zacchaeus himself, however, was delighted by the invitation. He responded to Jesus immediately, climbing down from his perch, as Jesus had called him to do. And not only did Zacchaeus receive Jesus into his home, it appears he received him into his heart as well because the impact of this encounter with Jesus transformed Zacchaeus' life, completely. He vowed to give half of his possessions to the poor and to pay back those he had cheated (four times as much as he had taken), and so, it happened that, in meeting Jesus and encountering his love, Zacchaeus' selfish soul was somehow healed. No longer oriented towards the question of 'how much can I *get*?' but to the question of 'how much can I *give*?'

We read that Jesus said to him: 'Today salvation has come to this house' (Luke 19.9, NIV). Salvation means freedom. Soul freedom. And a relationship with God that goes on for ever. What's fascinating about this is that salvation, in some other religions, is something that you earn, something you work towards by means of good words and good deeds. But what is crystal clear from this Bible story is that Zacchaeus did not deserve salvation. His life did not merit God's love. Nonetheless, he received it, as a gift of *grace*, when he opened his heart to Jesus.

Interestingly, this is one of the things one discovers when one starts reading the Bible, that this theme of grace – of getting what you do not deserve – is the recurring message of the book. The picture the Bible paints is that, although God desires all people to live morally good lives, there is grace when we fall, for those who are willing, as Zacchaeus was, to receive that grace and forgiveness.

We might say, then, that Zacchaeus the tax collector discovered in the person of Jesus Christ: (1) a reason to be good, (2) help to be good and (3) grace in his failings. While we may never have cheated in life or in business as spectacularly as Zacchaeus did – or maybe we have – are not all of us in need of these three things as well?

4

The matter of truth

Does truth exist, and does it matter?

Is ultimate truth ultimately knowable?

Thinking about life's big questions – questions of meaning, purpose, value and goodness – is part of what it means to be human. However, while many are searching for answers to these questions, others have concluded that there are no answers; or that even if the answers do exist, we will never know what they are.

From my experience of speaking on university campuses, this scepticism is a prevailing mood in academia – the view that even if there are answers to these important questions, they are beyond our reach to grasp. The great French thinker Blaise Pascal came to a similar view over 300 years ago. Born in France in 1623, he was a renowned mathematician, philosopher and scientist. To give but one example of his genius, while he was still a teenager, Pascal invented a calculating machine that was to become the earliest fore-runner of the modern computer.

He struggled with his health for many years and only lived to see his thirty-ninth year. But throughout his life, Pascal thought very deeply about the big questions of life, including the question of God. As a philosopher, Pascal had reasoned, as many postmodern thinkers do today, that because we are finite beings it is somewhat silly, even arrogant, to think we can speak with any certainty about the nature of ultimate reality, including the existence of God. He famously described humans as beings who find themselves suspended between an infinity above (at the astronomical level) and an infinity below (at the atomic level). Knowledge of ultimate reality, he argued, must therefore remain forever beyond our limited reach.

However, Pascal was also a Christian. Shortly after his death, a manuscript was found sewn inside his jacket pocket. On the manuscript were inscribed some of Pascal's thoughts describing his profound conversion to Christianity that had occurred eight years prior, including the following: 'Not the God of the philosophers and scholars but the God of Abraham, Isaac and Jacob'.

Not the God of the philosophers . . .

What did Pascal mean by these words? Did he mean that Christianity was somehow anti-philosophical? Did he mean that thoughtful and intelligent people, people like philosophers, couldn't possibly believe in the God of the Bible?

He meant neither of these things. He himself was a philosopher and, indeed, many, if not most, of the brightest minds of Pascal's day understood a designer God to be the best explanation for the existence of this amazing universe we inhabit (with its over-whelming impression of order and design); and for the existence of human beings as well (given our consciousness, rationality, morality, spiritual longings and propensity to worship).

Rather, what Pascal meant by his statement – not the God of the philosophers – was this: that God is much more than just an abstract philosophical concept. He is more than just the 'first cause' or 'prime mover' that philosophers sometimes identify as the origin of this universe. Pascal had come to the radical conclusion that God is actually a person. That he is relational. That he is someone who knows us by name and someone with whom we can have a relationship.

Which begs the question: if Pascal reasoned that our finite nature means that knowledge of ultimate reality lies forever beyond human discovering, why did he adhere to Christianity? Why did *he* maintain that God was behind it all? Was it merely on a whim or simply on the basis of cultural tradition or social convention that he remained a Christian? Was his Christianity just a lifestyle choice? Did he have to leave his philosophical brain at the door when he went to church? No, none of these things was the case. You see, Pascal didn't say it was impossible for us to know ultimate reality, he said it was impossible for us to know ultimate reality *on our own*.

But *what if*, he reasoned, ultimate reality is ultimately personal and wants to be known? That, he realized, would be a complete and utter game-changer. Because then it would be possible for us finite beings to know ultimate reality. And in fact, that's the view that Pascal finally came to: God himself – ultimate reality, the Creator of the universe – wants to be known and has revealed himself to us by entering into our space-time human history, as he did in the times of Abraham, Isaac and Jacob, and as he did most clearly and intimately in and through Jesus Christ.

A meaningful answer

Lewis made a similar point in his response to the comments Yuri Gagarin made about God after returning to earth as the first man in space. The Russian cosmonaut reportedly announced to the world that his atheism was justified because he had been into outer space and had not seen any God. Lewis's brilliant response was that this was like Hamlet going into the attic of his castle looking for Shakespeare. Lewis's point was that if God exists, we are not going to find him simply by looking under every rock, on top of every mountain or even behind every planet in the solar system. Why not? Because, reasoned Lewis, God is not merely a character in the play; he is the Playwright himself. He is not just another life in the universe but the Author of life itself, the Creator of this universe.

But *what if*? What if the Great Playwright, the Author of life, wanted to make himself known to us, the characters in his story, just as Pascal suggested was possible, how could that work?

Lewis asks us to imagine for a moment that William Shakespeare wanted to reveal his existence to Hamlet. Could he do that? Yes, he could, in at least one of two ways. He could either write clues about himself into the play, pointing Hamlet to his existence; or, even more intimately, he could actually write himself into the play, becoming both author and character at the same time.

Pascal (and Lewis) believed that the God of the Bible had done both of these things for us; as do many leading thinkers today, including world-class philosophers, Nobel-prize winning scientists and respected historians.

'Two things fill me with ever increasing awe', wrote the philosopher Immanuel Kant, 'the starry heavens above me and the moral law within me'.

Christians believe that God has written clues about himself into the very fabric of our existence, both in this dazzlingly beautiful and complex world which we inhabit and in the equally beautiful, yet complex inner world of our own human intuitions, longings and experiences. They both tell a story.

But in addition to these tremendous clues without and within (which we will examine in greater detail in the next chapters), Christianity claims that God has also written himself into history. In the person of Jesus Christ, God himself, we are told, entered into our space-time human history and became one of us. A human being. And not just any human being, but the main character in human history. In an article in *Time* magazine in 2013, it was said that of all the people who have ever walked the face of this planet, this Jewish carpenter from Nazareth named Jesus has left the biggest historical footprint of all (something else we will consider more closely in the chapters to come).

That is one of the remarkable things about Christianity. Many have tried to dismiss it as little more than a myth or fairy tale. But when you read about the life of Jesus in the Bible, you see that it is unlike the stories of the gods of myth and legend whose adventures and exploits have no contact with human history. You see that Jesus actually lived in a place we can visit at a time in history we can study. You will read of Herod and Judea, Caesar Augustus, and the Roman Empire. In other words, these are real people, real places, real events and real history. And unlike any fairy tale, Christianity's claims can be objectively investigated because it makes claims about events that have happened in the real world. Our world.

Public truth

Consider, for example, what historians tell us about the life of the followers of Jesus in the years following his crucifixion. Those who saw how followers of the early Church were treated must have wondered why anyone would willingly choose to be a follower of Jesus. They were persecuted for their faith by the Roman authorities. What is interesting, though, is that Jesus' followers needn't have been persecuted at all. After all, Roman society was a relatively tolerant, religiously pluralistic society. One could walk through a Roman town and encounter the widest variety of religious temples to worship in and philosophies to embrace. The Empire accepted and even encouraged such a diversity of beliefs and expressions. Why then were the Christians in particular persecuted, excluded and even fed to the lions for their faith?

To understand this, one needs to know that religion in Rome fell into either one of two categories: *cultus privatus* (private religion) or *cultus publicus* (public religion). A private religion meant a religion whose teaching and ideas were held to be true for the members of that particular religious community. A public religion meant a religion that was held to be true for everyone. There were many different private religions in the Roman Empire, but according to law, there could be only one public religion, only one religion that was held to be true and was to be followed by everyone, and that religion was the worship of Caesar.

For most people, that was considered a fair enough deal and they kept to the rules. But then along came the early Christians with a message of good news about Jesus Christ which they claimed was not just true for Christians but true for everyone. They refused to treat this news about Jesus Christ as merely a private truth and were also unwilling to bow down and worship Caesar as Lord of all. Therefore, they came into conflict with the state, with almighty Caesar himself.

The reason that the early Christians believed that the good news of Jesus Christ's life, death and resurrection was unavoidably public truth was because it was more than simply an idea to believe, an ideal to strive for or a value to uphold. To them, the good news was an objective historical *fact.* Jesus had clearly demonstrated his Lordship in his life, teachings and miracles, and most supremely, in his resurrection. He had claimed he would rise from the dead and, according to his disciples, he literally – that is, factually – did so.

The disciples had been eyewitnesses of these historical events, and the thing about an historical event is that it is, by definition, public truth in the sense that it is true for everyone, whether we like it or not, and whether it conveniently fits into our pre-existing worldviews or not. One can choose not to believe that an historical event happened, but if it did happen, our private refusal to believe it does not alter the public fact that it did.

For the early Christians, not only was the news about Jesus public truth, it was also truth that should be shared publicly because to them, it was exceedingly good news, and it would be unloving not to share it with others. And so, having been witnesses to these wonderful events – particularly the resurrection, which to the early Christians spelt 'H-O-P-E' – they couldn't in all conscience just keep the good news to themselves.

Interestingly, Christians still face persecution today in some parts of the world for their refusal to stop promoting this 'good news' about Jesus as public truth, usually from totalitarian govern-ments or totalitarian religious groups who wish to control what people can and can't believe. Unfortunately, the Church has also been guilty of doing this at various times in history, such as during the Inquisition, but whenever it has, it has done so in direct viola-tion of the very teachings of Christ himself.

Even today in so-called liberal, tolerant and democratic soci-eties, people who believe in God still face pressure of various kinds to keep their faith private. Lesslie Newbigin, a priest who ministered most of his life in India, on returning to the UK in his later years, made an interesting point about the modern Western idea of diversity and tolerance that had arisen in his absence. He observed that if two scientists who are conducting the same experiment in their laboratories, with the same materials, under the same conditions, end up producing contradictory results, they do not embrace each other and say, 'what a joy it is to live in a diverse and pluralist society!' Rather, they go on discussing and evaluating the matter until either one or both of them are proved wrong in their conclusions. By contrast, he said, to believe that something is true for everyone in the realm of religious belief and to attempt to convince others that it is true, that is regarded as arrogant, intolerant, an attempt to dominate, or even an improper intrusion into the privacy of another person's life. Why the different responses? Because, he observed, whereas we believe that science deals in the realm of facts, we believe that religion deals in the realm of values, and one must not impose one's values on someone else.

But as Newbigin observed, this fact/value dichotomy is simply wrong, at least when it comes to Christianity. That's because even though Christianity has values, it is not primarily about values, it's about facts. As we have seen, Christianity has to do with real things that God has done in human history. Things that can be objectively investigated and discussed.

For example, the apostle John spoke about faith in the Lord Jesus in the context of that 'which we have heard, which we have seen with our eyes, which we have looked at and our hands have touched' (1 John 1.1, NIV). Luke wrote at the beginning of his Gospel account of Jesus that the Christian message depends on that which has been 'fulfilled among us . . . handed down by those who from the first were eyewitnesses and servants of [Jesus]' (Luke 1.2, NIV). The apostle Paul in his letters to the churches spoke about events in Jewish history that provided examples for believers in the first century.

Christianity is full of historical, factual claims. And just like the example of the two scientists who investigate together their different findings of fact, we can discuss the factual claims that Christianity makes and subject those claims to rigorous intellectual scrutiny. It may be that we end up disagreeing about the truth of those factual claims, but just because two people might disagree with each other doesn't mean that either of them has to be disagreeable with each other in the process. Believe it or not, it is possible for even the best of friends to disagree on claims about truth that really matter. And, after all, the more we are willing to discuss the things that matter together, the more likely we are, much like the scientific endeavour, to affirm gradually what is true and let go of what is not.

Does truth matter?

Today, however, there are increasing numbers of people who don't really believe that truth or 'the facts' matter at all. Whereas Newbigin's analogy about the two scientists assumes that we live in a society that is interested in the truth of things, culturally we seem to be moving off in a direction that makes such an assumption somewhat uncertain.

In 2016, *The Economist* magazine published an influential article arguing that the West has become a post-truth society. In other words, a society where public opinion is influenced far more by appeals to emotion and personal opinion than by appeals to objective facts. And you may recall that at the end of that year, the *Oxford English Dictionary* announced that 'Post-truth' was their word of the year.

The renowned Canadian philosopher, Charles Taylor, has described our modern Western society as disenchanted. He calls it disenchanted because the view of the intellectual establishment is that we no longer believe in anything transcendent. We don't believe in absolutes. God used to be regarded as one of those absolutes. No longer. Objective truth used to be regarded as one of those absolutes. No longer.

'Is truth dead?' That was the provocative question on the front cover of *Time* magazine in March of 2017, very much resembling the famous *Time* cover of 1966: 'Is God dead?' In a world of fake news, alternative facts, political correctness and thinly veiled tribalism – it is a question many are presently wondering.

And to top it off, there is cultural confusion when it comes to the notion of truth.

You see, on the one hand, you have the academic world and, in it, the popular view of truth is that it is relative, cultural, socially constructed. There is no such thing as absolute or objective truth, only people's personal opinions and perspectives. What is true for one individual or one culture is true for them but not necessarily for anyone else.

On the other hand, you have everyday life and common sense. In everyday life, truth seems anything but relative. Whether we are receiving an itemized bill from the mechanic telling us what needed to be fixed or reading a bank statement to see how much money is in our bank account, whether we are testifying in court or getting a structural survey done on a house or visiting the doctor, we don't live as if truth were relative. We don't live as if it didn't matter or it didn't exist. We don't live as if one view were just as legitimate as any other.

Why not? Because we know, from reason and experience, that truth matters.

Not so long ago, my then four-year-old daughter Grace woke me up to tell me that my then three-year-old son Jonathan had hurt himself. When I went into their bedroom, I found Jonathan on the floor unable to walk, unable to use his legs. Because he had been having high temperatures for a few days, it was very possible that whatever was causing him to be unable to walk was very serious indeed and so we were quickly on our way to the hospital.

It was a great relief when the hospital paediatrician finally came to us with the news that although the fever had resulted in some muscle breakdown in his legs, it wasn't anything more sinister than that, and with plenty of rest and fluid he was going to be well and able to walk again soon.

Is truth dead? Does truth matter?

In the case of my son, Jonathan, as I waited in that hospital room for the results of his blood test, the answer was obvious. Yes. The truth matters. I wasn't looking for different ideas, perspectives, thoughts or feelings about what was ailing him. I was looking for a diagnosis. I was looking for authority. I was looking for the truth.

Unavoidable truth

In responding to those who would argue that truth is relative, the Oxford philosopher Roger Scruton wrote: '[Somebody] who says that there are no truths, or that all truth is "merely relative", is asking you not to believe them. So don't!'

That, I want to suggest, is the essential problem for those who hold that there is no truth. On the one hand, they say that truth doesn't exist. On the other hand, they are claiming that it is true that truth doesn't exist. It's a logical contradiction. A contradiction unfortunately that many people fail to see; that is, until reality bites them, and reminds them that truth exists whether we like it or not.

It reminds me of an apparently fictional but nonetheless humorous story that I delightedly discovered one day on the BBC's Scottish website, about a radio conversation said to have taken place between the British and Irish off the coast of County Kerry, Ireland. The conversation reads as follows:

Irish: Please divert your course 15 degrees to the south to avoid a collision.

British: Recommend you divert your course 15 degrees to the north to avoid a collision.

Irish: Negative. You will have to divert your course 15 degrees to the south to avoid a collision.

British: This is the captain of a British navy ship, I say again divert YOUR course.

Irish: Negative. I say again you will have to divert *your* course.

British: THIS IS THE AIRCRAFT CARRIER HMS *BRITANNIA*! THE SECOND LARGEST SHIP IN THE BRITISH ATLANTIC FLEET. WE ARE ACCOMPANIED BY THREE DESTROYERS, THREE CRUISERS AND NUMEROUS SUPPORT VESSELS. I DEMAND YOU CHANGE YOUR COURSE 15 DEGREES NORTH, I SAY AGAIN, THAT IS 15 DEGREES NORTH OR COUNTERMEASURES WILL BE TAKEN TO ENSURE THE SAFETY OF THIS SHIP.

Irish: We are a lighthouse. Your call.

I want to suggest that truth is very much like that lighthouse in the story. It exists whether you want to acknowledge it or not. And you ignore it at your own peril. As Dallas Willard wryly observes: 'Reality is what you run into when you're wrong.'

Other things in life are just matters of opinion or perspective. For example, the question of which tastes better, Coke Zero or Pepsi Max? Or which is the better holiday, a week at the beach or a week of rock climbing? There's no necessarily right or wrong answer, unless you're my wife, in which case the correct answer is the beach. But really, the answers to these things are just matters of preference.

Other questions, however, are a matter of reality, a question of fact: is this fizzy drink good for my health or not? Will this rope hold my weight or not? Is that a small boat ahead . . . or a lighthouse?

Many people think that the big religious and philosophical questions of life are merely questions of preference or taste, in the same category as the questions, 'What's your favourite drink?' or 'Where's your favourite holiday?' But they aren't. They are questions of fact.

Are we here by accident or here on purpose? Is there a right and wrong way to live? Is there life after death? Do I have a soul? Is there a God? These are questions of fact. There either is a life after death, or there isn't. There either is a God, or there isn't. Jesus Christ is either risen from the dead and alive today, or he isn't.

Now, as individuals with freedom of choice, we all need to make our own decisions about these important questions, each person must think, investigate and decide for themselves, but the one thing we cannot say is that the truth doesn't matter.

Some decisions we make in life matter for a day or a week or a year. Other choices matter for a lifetime. But when it comes to the big questions, such as the question of God – this is a choice that matters for eternity.

Lewis put it like this: 'Christianity is a statement which, if false, is of no importance and, if true, of infinite importance. The one thing it cannot be is moderately important.' For the same reason, Pascal also concluded that if you were a gambler, it would be unreasonable for you to decide not to at least consider and investigate Christianity, seriously, because there's absolutely nothing to lose by investigating and yet possibly everything to gain.

But to take something like Christianity and say: 'Well, it's either true, or it isn't true', doesn't go down well in today's cultural climate – not only because truth is thought to be relative or subjective, but also because claims of objective truth are thought to be offensive. Speaking of objective truth has come to be regarded by many as an act of aggression.

Truth and tolerance

How has this come about? A popular view of truth has developed which holds that all our beliefs and ideas have been socially constructed, and usually constructed by those in power. Therefore, overarching claims about truth are viewed with great suspicion, as attempts to dominate and suppress individual freedom. And nothing is more highly valued in the West than individual freedom.

Claims about truth imply that anyone who thinks differently is wrong, but to say that people are wrong is to deprive them of their right to feel affirmed about the things they feel strongly about. And we all have the right to feel affirmed, right? The result of this type of thinking, though – however well motivated it might be – is that we no longer feel comfortable talking in public about what we take to be true anymore because we are afraid that, in doing so, we might offend someone.

We pride ourselves on being a tolerant society. Tolerance used to mean something like the comment attributed to Voltaire: 'I disapprove of what you say, but I will defend to the death your right to say it.' That was the old understanding of tolerance. The new understanding of tolerance, as D. A. Carson points out, means by contrast: 'I cannot, will not, and dare not disapprove of what you say, because what you have to say is every bit as valid as what I have to say. And I will put to death anyone who says otherwise.'

In other words, the new tolerance tolerates not only all people but all ideas. To say that some ideas are right and others wrong is now intolerant, a form of abuse. And so, whatever is true for you is true for you, and whatever is true for me is true for me. But what we must never say is that something is true for everyone. That would be seen as a violation of our freedom to define the truth for ourselves. That would be intolerant; and in a post-truth world that rejects all certainties and all absolutes, one thing is absolutely certain: intolerance must not be tolerated.

The question of whether Jesus Christ was tolerant or intolerant is a very interesting one. You see, on the one hand, no one was off-limits from his love. Jesus loved all people, including some very unlovely ones. But on the other hand, he didn't love all ideas. Which is why what Jesus had to say is so incredibly jarring in today's world. Jesus didn't claim to be a truth, or one of a number of truths. He claimed to be the Truth.

In order for truth not to be ultimately relative there needs to be a fixed point from which everything else has reference, an ontic referent (to use the language of philosophers) or a North Star (to use the language of the poets). Jesus' claim was that he was that fixed point. That certain star. The ultimate source and arbiter of truth and reality.

He said, 'I am . . . the truth' (John 14.6, NIV). He also said, 'the truth shall set you free' (John 8.32, NIV).

Truth and freedom

That phrase (that the truth shall set you free) is the motto most commonly adopted by universities around the world. In the last few generations, however, the university has become a place where many have learned to devalue and distrust the notion of truth. Many have come to think of truth as something that, instead of promoting freedom, as Jesus suggested, in fact restrains us; limits us; boxes us in. Could this be one of the reasons why, as a society, we have walked away from truth? Could it be because, deep down, we sense that truth might interfere with something that we long for even more? Freedom. Freedom without restraint or accountability.

The freedom to be able to do whatever we want, whenever we want, with whomever we want – without anyone or anything telling us otherwise?

Some atheist thinkers in their most open and revealing moments have admitted as much. Aldous Huxley, for example, writes:

> The philosopher who finds no meaning in the world is not concerned exclusively with a problem in pure metaphysics. He is also concerned to prove that there is no valid reason why he personally should not do as he wants to do. For myself, as no doubt for most of my friends, the philosophy of meaninglessness was essentially an instrument of liberation from a certain system of morality. We objected to the morality because it interfered with our sexual freedom.

Another atheist philosopher, Thomas Nagel, candidly writes:

> It isn't just that I don't believe in God and, naturally, hope that I'm right in my belief. It's that I hope there is no God! I don't want there to be a God; I don't want the universe to be like that. My guess is that this cosmic authority problem is not a rare condition . . .

In the *Time* magazine article, entitled 'Is truth dead?', the tone was not one of celebration but of warning. The key question the author asked was where we are headed as a society – socially, politically, culturally – if truth as a currency loses all value.

What happens to people who walk away from truth?

With respect to our university campuses, commentators on both sides of the political spectrum are lamenting the loss of free speech. Students are increasingly barring or no-platforming speakers who dare to speak their beliefs with certainty because that certainty is deemed to make those who don't share their beliefs feel uncomfortable, and everybody, we are told, has the right to feel comfortable on campus.

Many social commentators observing these events are asking whether we are not in fact losing our freedom in the name of freedom? Our freedom of speech. Our freedom to dissent. Our freedom simply to disagree.

Students correctly value inclusivity and non-discrimination and rightly feel moral outrage when these things are threatened. But if all truth is relative, as many students believe, then one must ask, where does this moral outrage come from? If it is based on students' rights, then where do those rights come from? Because without truth, there are no rights to speak of; because without truth there is no right or wrong.

When we experience moral outrage over certain injustices or over the violation of a person's dignity, it is a clue that truth, in this case moral truth, really exists. Because it makes no sense for a person to be outraged over something unless he or she really believes, deep down, that that something is absolutely, truly, objectively wrong.

The problem with trying to dismiss claims about truth as nothing more than attempts to exercise power over other people is that by removing truth we are actually removing the only thing that can speak up against abusive power because, as Nietzsche pointed out long ago, if truth doesn't exist, then power is all there is.

It was the general belief in the existence of truth that allowed people like Martin Luther King, Jr; Nelson Mandela; Václav Havel and Desmond Tutu to speak truth to power. Truth was all they had at their disposal in their ultimately successful fights for freedom against oppressive laws and regimes.

'One word of truth outweighs the entire world', wrote the novelist Aleksandr Solzhenitsyn, himself a victim of totalitarian regimes. But if we no longer believe in truth, then we are in trouble, socially and politically, because we can no longer recognize a lie.

And as the journalist Walter Lippmann sagely observed: 'There can be no liberty for a community which lacks the means to detect lies.'

Truth is an absolutely essential requirement for freedom. No truth, no freedom. 'Then you will know the truth,' said Jesus, 'and the truth will set you free' (John 8.32, NIV). That's demonstrably true not only at the political level, but also at the personal level.

I once heard an amusing tale about a little boy who had lots of pretty marbles. But this boy was constantly eyeing his sister's bagful of sweets. One day, he said to her: 'If you give me all your sweets, I'll give you all of my marbles.' She gave it much thought and agreed to the trade. He took all her sweets and went back to his room to get his marbles, but the more he admired them, the more reluctant he became to give them all up. So, he hid the best of them under his pillow and took the rest to her. That night, she slept soundly, while he tossed and turned restlessly, unable to sleep and thinking to himself: 'I wonder if she gave me all the sweets?'

As the story reveals, truth brings freedom, whereas lies lead to captivity or slavery – on the inside. Of course, we prefer freedom to slavery, but the problem is that we don't always prefer the truth to its opposite. Why is that? Why do we have such an uneasy relationship with truth?

Uncomfortable truth

Aristotle once asked his readers to imagine a morally perfect person, a sort of God among us. Someone who was morally pure, but who could also look into people's eyes and see everything that they had ever thought, said and done. 'What would a society do with a such a person?' Aristotle asked. It would ostracize or even kill such a God-like being.

Why? Well, how would you feel in the presence of someone who is at all times morally perfect and, at the same time, able to see all your moral imperfections, including the ones that no one else can see? Perfectly at ease? I doubt it. I know I wouldn't be. I would want to wear a pair of dark sunglasses around a person like that.

Why the instinct to hide? If we are honest with ourselves, we all have parts of our character, our feelings, our thoughts and our actions that we would prefer people not to see. Things about us which (we are afraid) would put people off or make them feel offended, maybe even disgusted, should they ever find out. The truth can be incredibly uncomfortable.

Jesus speaks about this when he says, 'light has come into the world, but people loved darkness instead of light' (John 3.19, NIV). As Christian speaker Michael Ramsden points out, darkness might not be pleasant, but it allows things to stay hidden. The problem with light is that it reveals things as they really are.

Jesus' friends and followers believed Jesus was morally perfect, literally God among men. A man who knew what was in every human heart. An incredible thing when you consider they lived and travelled with Jesus 24/7 for three years. Jesus himself said: 'I am the light of the world' (John 8.12, NIV). We should therefore expect that he would have made a lot of people feel uncomfortable, and when you read about him in the Bible, you see that he really did. People tried to ostracize him and when that didn't work, they eventually had him arrested and killed on false charges.

However, there were also many who loved him. How was it then, that Jesus' friends, those who loved him, were able to withstand the gaze of someone who knew all truth, who could see into the very depths of their soul, who knew everything they ever did and everything they ever thought, and not be afraid?

The answer the Bible gives us is 'love'. The Bible says that 'perfect love drives out all fear' (1 John 4.18, NIV); and that Jesus not only has the ability to shine a light into the depths of your soul and to see the real you, including the dark places in your soul, but also loves you entirely and cannot help but love you with an everlasting love.

Truth and love

In other words, this light that reveals the shadows in your heart also has the power to send those shadows fleeing. For this light, which is truth, not only exposes, it also heals; for it is just as much the light of love as it is the light of truth. Truth full of love and love full of truth – and not merely conceptually, but personally, relationally – in Jesus Christ, the light of the world, the Son of God.

Today, we often say that the greatest virtue is tolerance. But if you were to ask people 100 years ago what the greatest virtue was, they would have answered 'love'. Tolerance is a poor substitute for love, and that is why we would all prefer to hear the words 'I love you' rather than 'I tolerate you'. The poet Criss Jami writes that tolerance is patience that no longer has hope and love which has given up. Chesterton describes what we call tolerance as 'the appalling frenzy of the indifferent'.

According to the Christian faith, God does not merely tolerate us, nor is he indifferent towards us. The Bible says that God loves us, and we are, each of us, his treasure. He sees our hearts, as they truly are, without ever rejecting us. And through Jesus he offers to forgive us for the wrongs we have done and rescue us from the dark sides of our character – our selfishness, addictions, shame and guilt.

In other words, Christianity claims to offer us true freedom: not simply the freedom to live however we please – which is a negative freedom (freedom from), but the freedom to live as we were created to live – which is a positive freedom (freedom for). And it claims we need the light of God's truth to help us fully discern the life we were created to live; and the light of his love to fill us and enable us to live fully, as we were created to live. Thus, it is an invitation to know and experience this truth and love, not just as a religion or philosophy, but also as a relationship with the one who is the source of all truth and love – Jesus Christ.

If all of the above is true, then we should receive this invitation as good news, provided, of course, we don't mind the implication that we need to be rescued. But if we are honest, we don't always like the idea of needing to be rescued.

I remember the utter embarrassment that I felt as a seven-year-old boy, when I needed to be rescued from being dragged out to sea. I was on a small blow-up canoe at the beach and struggling to paddle back to shore against the tide that was pulling me away from it. If two teenaged girls hadn't noticed my predicament and helped me, I would have been dragged out to sea. Now, I didn't want to be dragged out to sea, but I didn't want to be rescued either, especially by two girls! It was so embarrassing. I didn't want to acknowledge the truth: that I needed their help. I told them to leave me alone, that I didn't need their help. But thankfully they ignored my pride and brought me safely back to shore.

I have discovered that, in life, we need both truth and love. We need someone who can tell us the truth about our situation – you're in trouble, you need help, rescuing. And we need someone who is actually willing to help us. We need a teacher who can tell us what we don't know, but we also need a teacher who is willing to help us learn what we should know. We need a coach who can tell us where we are playing badly, and we also need a coach who is willing to invest in us the time we need to become better. We need a doctor who can diagnose accurately, and we also need a doctor who is willing to get his or her hands bloody and operate on us.

If you study the life and teachings of Jesus Christ, you find both of these things. There is truth – we are told we are far more lost, spiritually and morally, than we could ever have imagined. So, we need to be rescued. Yet, there is also love – we discover that we are far more precious to God than we could ever have imagined. So, he has come to rescue us, at great cost to himself.

I once heard a story about a little girl whose parents warned her, time and time again, that she should never wander off into the

71

woods that bordered their little farm because it was dangerous and easy to get lost in. But one day, the little girl decided that she would explore all the dark secrets of the forest. The farther she wandered, the denser it became, until she lost her bearings and could not find her way back. As darkness descended, fear gripped her, and all her screams and sobs only made her feel weary until she fell asleep in the woods. Friends, family and volunteers combed the area but gave up in the thick of the night. All except for her father who continued to search. Early the next morning, the girl awoke to the first ray of sunlight to see her dad running towards her as fast as he could. She threw her arms out to him and, as he wrapped her up in his tight embrace, she repeated over and over: 'Daddy, I found you!'

That which our hearts most desperately seek – to be fully known, yet fully loved – is, according to the Christian story, ultimately found in a person who has already sought each of us, Jesus Christ. Of course, whether or not this story is true is a question we all need to investigate for ourselves; just as whether or not we are interested in truth is something we need to decide for ourselves. That being said, regardless of whether we are interested in truth, according to the Christian story, the Truth is very much interested in us.

5

The matter of love
Is there a love that will never let me down?

The greatest thing in the world

Imagine for a moment, if you can, that we all suddenly discovered we only had five minutes left to live. What would we do? We would all be on the phone calling the people who are dear to us and telling them that we love them. So argues the essayist and poet Christopher Morley, citing this thought experiment as proof that life without love is meaningless. No matter how recognized we become or how many great accomplishments we achieve, they are no substitute for love.

It was the German poet Novalis who wrote of love as being 'the Amen of the universe'. Similarly, the Scottish biologist and evangelist Henry Drummond spoke of love as the greatest thing in the world.

We celebrate love, we value love, we long for love. But as the Eurodance artist Haddaway once asked in his famous hit song of the same name: 'What is love?'

According to Google analytics, this question – what is love? – is one of the most frequently asked question on the Internet. Part of the confusion stems from the fact that we use the word love in so many different contexts. I can say: 'I love chocolate. I love cricket. I love my dog. I love my wife.' But hopefully, I mean something different in each case.

What is love? Real love?

According to a popular anecdote, a group of social scientists once posed this very same question to a group of four- to eight-year olds. These were some of the children's answers:

When my grandmother got arthritis, she couldn't bend over and paint her toenails any more. So my grandfather does it for her all the time, even when his hands got arthritis too. That's love.
(Rebecca, age 8)

Love is what's in the room with you at Christmas if you stop opening presents and listen.
(Bobby, age 7)

Love is like a little old woman and a little old man who are still friends even after they know each other so well.
(Tommy, age 6)

Love is when Mummy gives Daddy the best piece of chicken.
(Elaine, age 5)

Love is when Mummy sees Daddy smelly and sweaty and still says he is handsomer than George Clooney.
(Chris, age 7)

These are some great definitions of love. It seems to me that children often intuitively have a better handle on what love is than many of today's so-called experts on the topic.

Modern love

According to psychiatrist Dr Larry Young, 'love is simply a cocktail of chemicals operating in the brain to give us the sensation of love'. Similarly, science commentator Jim Al-Khalili suggests that, biologically speaking, 'love is a powerful neurological condition like hunger or thirst, only more permanent'. He further explains, 'We talk about love being blind or unconditional, in the sense that we have no control over it. But then, that is not so surprising since love is basically chemistry.'

In other words, contrary to the understanding of many of history's great thinkers on the subject of love – Aristotle, Augustine, Shakespeare, Dostoevsky – who recognized and spoke of a mysterious beauty, sacredness and transcendence in love – modern culture has largely reduced love to a physical phenomenon. A biological appetite. Like hunger or thirst.

We see an apple, we feel hungry, so we eat it. We see a person, we feel love, so we . . . what? We love them. But how, why? What does that mean if love is just a physical appetite in need of satisfaction?

One of the well-known songlines from Jim Morrison and his band The Doors is from their classic, 'Hello, I love you'. The bit, '. . . won't you tell me your name?' makes it a funny line and it's a catchy song. But it raises a question: can you really love someone you don't know? The answer given by your grandmother's grandmother would have been, 'Of course not,' recognizing that we cannot be truly loved if we are not truly known. But in a culture in which we understand love as a physical appetite, to believe that you can love someone you don't know actually makes complete sense because then it's just about what I feel. It's completely subjective. It's my feelings. It's my appetite.

However, the thing about appetites is that sometimes they can come on very quickly but, equally, they can disappear very quickly or attach themselves to another object just as quickly. Appetites come and go. Feelings come and go.

But if love really is nothing more than a physical phenomenon over which we have no control, why do we feel the need within our hearts for a love that will never leave us nor ever forsake us?

Will you still love me tomorrow?

Tom Wolfe famously described the modern understanding of love as nothing more than a cult of the self and the unleashing of its urges. Dr Elizabeth Lasch-Quinn diagnoses the modern lover today as 'a singleton, lacking emotional depth, living for the day, shying away from commitment that might curtail his personal growth and viewing other people as instruments to be manipulated in his own quest for fulfilment'.

We see the inevitable insecurity that this modern approach to love naturally engenders in the words of a song by Carole King written some decades ago but still popular today: 'Will you still love me tomorrow?'

Her song begins with all the romance and sensuality that many of us have come to expect from Soul music. She sings of her lover's sweet love and that for tonight, he is all hers. But then the question starts to rise: Will you still love me tomorrow? As King continues to sing, tonight's pleasure is filled with questions about tomorrow; is this pleasure for a moment or is it lasting? Former experiences, perhaps, cause her to question whether her lover is telling her the truth when he says she is the only one for him. She cannot help but ask herself whether her heart will be broken when the night passes and the morning comes. Essentially, she asks . . . Will you still love me tomorrow?

It's a deep question of the heart – a question to which we hope the answer will be 'yes'. However, if love really is nothing more than some chemistry and neurology over which we have no control, then on what basis can anyone promise to still love someone tomorrow, let alone, for better or for worse, for richer or for poorer, in sickness and in health, until death do us part?

In a world that is constantly reducing everything important to mere biology and chemistry, we have got to ask ourselves: 'Is anything important anymore? Is anything sacred?' Or conversely: 'Is even love not sacred anymore?'

Losing our awareness of the sacredness of love led to the invention or description of a new type of love in the twentieth century, the idea of 'free love'. The term, popularized by thinkers of the 1960s and 70s, came to denote the idea of love without commitment – love without cost, sacrifice or conditions. However, as Chesterton pointed out, free love is actually a contradiction in terms. For it is the nature of real love to commit; it is the nature of love to sacrifice; it is the nature of love to protect. Chesterton writes: '[A]s if a real lover ever had been or ever could be free. It is the nature of love to bind itself.' If we are honest, what passes for love today is often best described as self-gratification or indulgence rather than love.

There is a book in the Bible called the Song of Songs. It celebrates the beauty of love between two lovers, the man and the woman, Solomon and his bride. It's a very sensual book – but it's also a very spiritual book. Sex and spirituality overlap in a powerful way. And we see here that love between the lovers includes the physical joining together of two bodies, with all the pleasurable neurochemical reactions that surround that attraction and connection. But it also explains that the love that they share is much more than just the physical dimension. It is also the binding or knitting together of two souls, the becoming of one in heart and spirit, which reflects something truly awesome about the way that God, who is Spirit, loves – not with a compulsive, self-gratifying, self-indulgent love; but with a freely given, self-giving, self-sacrificing love that both delights in the other and commits itself to the other.

This is a love that is not conditional on neurochemical reactions or subjective feelings alone. It is a love that proceeds from the spirit or will of a person. A love that chooses to say: 'Whether better times or worse times come, I will never leave you nor ever forsake you.'

A love that never fails

Christianity says that, at the heart of the universe, one finds real love, not the cold indifference of mindless atoms and soulless chemicals, but love.

'God is love', says the Bible.

Philosophers speak of God as the first cause of the universe. The one who set everything in motion. The unmoved mover. But in Christianity we see that God is not merely a necessary philosophical abstraction; he is a person who loves that which he has brought into being. The Bible says God is love, not because love is God but because God's primary characteristic is love. He didn't just invent love, he embodies it.

Thus, if Christianity is true, it means that love is not merely a concept, a compulsion or a chemical reaction, but something concrete, something real – rooted and grounded in the being of the Creator of the universe. It means that God is the ultimate source of love and, therefore, the objective reference point for understanding what real love is.

And if that's true, then it places the whole story of our existence in a completely new light, for it means the reason behind your existence and mine is not luck but love. Not blind, indifferent and random chance, but a fierce, determined and purposeful love. It's a completely unique and radically different picture of reality. As I once heard a preacher put it, in every other faith or worldview, life precedes love, only in the Christian faith does love precede life.

There is an illustrated children's Bible called the *Storybook Bible* written by Sally Lloyd Jones. My children have a copy of it, and I sometimes read it to them as they are going to sleep. Rather memorably, it describes God's love as 'Never Stopping, Never Giving Up, Unbreaking, Always and Forever Love'. It is the opposite of the sort of love that leaves one wondering, 'Will you still love me tomorrow?' It is the sort of love that allows souls to lay themselves bare in the presence of the one who loves, without fear of scorn or rejection.

Recall, as I mentioned in Chapter 2, the apostle Paul's description of what perfect love – God's love – looks like. It's recorded in the Bible in a letter from Paul to the church in Corinth. To summarize, he writes that:

Love is patient and kind, not envious or boastful or proud, not dishonouring or self-seeking, not easily angered. It keeps no record of wrongs. Love delights not in evil but rejoices with the truth. Love always protects, always trusts, always hopes, always perseveres. Love never fails.

God's love never fails.

For many of us, a love like that is hard to imagine. Too often we are hurt the most by the very people who should have loved us the most. And too often we fail to love others as we ought to love them. Both types of experiences can be hugely painful. Few things in life are crueller than rejection or remorse.

Peter was one of Jesus' closest disciples. Peter thought that he loved his friend and teacher with a perfect love; one that would never fail. So much so, that on the night Jesus was arrested, Peter boldly announced that even if he had to die, he would never abandon Jesus. But after Jesus was arrested, the disciples scattered, and Peter (who had promised that even if the others fell away, he would never do so) disowned Jesus publicly, not once, but three times, the minute he was asked if he, too, was a follower of Jesus. Soon after his denial, Peter was racked with remorse. He broke down in tears. But what could he do? Jesus was already in the hands of soldiers and police and, shortly thereafter, crucified.

So, Jesus was gone. Dead. Redemption seemed impossible. Love, it appears, had failed. Mercifully, however, this is not the end of the story, for Jesus – as we know – did not stay dead. The Bible records that, after his resurrection, Christ sought out Peter who had gone back to what he knew before he met Jesus: fishing.

Then, the resurrected Jesus appears to Peter and his companions on the beach. The men have a miraculous catch of fish. They gather around a fire and eat a wonderful meal of barbecued fish and bread together. But afterwards, Jesus takes Peter aside and has a personal conversation with him. And in this conversation Jesus asks Peter:

'Do you love me?' And Peter says, 'Yes, Lord, I love you.' Then Jesus asks again: 'Do you love me?' Peter responds: 'Yes I love you.' And when Jesus asks a third time, the Bible records that Peter was grieved. But we see that, in asking three times, Jesus was doing a wonderful thing. Peter had denied his love for Jesus three times, and Jesus now gives him the opportunity to confess his love three times, thereby restoring Peter to relationship. But not only does he restore him to relationship, he also restores him to a position of responsibility because Jesus – speaking of the other followers – replies to Peter each time he confesses his love: 'Feed my sheep. Feed my lambs. Feed my sheep.'

Jesus' love for Peter never failed, even though Peter's love for Jesus did. The story shows us how perfect love loves the other, both when they are lovely and when they are unlovely; when they are loving and not loving; when they deserve it and when they don't.

Not so long ago, my wife was sharing all that was going on in her heart with me. All the good and the bad and the ugly. And my wife is one of those people who is very gracious and forgiving to everyone except herself. At one point as she was sharing her struggles, she said: 'I just feel like my heart is so ugly.' And I was able to say to her, in all honesty, as she was sharing things she didn't feel proud of, that to me she had never seemed more beautiful. Because it really was so beautiful – her honesty and vulnerability. It is beautiful that we can be so transparent with each other. That I can share all the good and the bad with her, and she with me (and by the way, my bad is much worse than her bad and her good is much better than my good, so I really got the best deal there); and that neither of us has to worry about being rejected because we have vowed never to leave or forsake each other, for better or for worse. We have discovered that in that soil of trust and of commitment to each other, the finest blooms of love can grow, and continue to grow, year after year.

Marriage is meant to be a place where two souls can be naked with each other, where they don't have to be afraid or hide. But according to Christianity, it's not the only place where one is meant to find a 'Never Stopping, Never Giving Up, Unbreaking, Always and Forever Love'. It is meant to exist in all sorts of loving human relationships.

A picture of God's love

The Bible does not only compare God's love to the love between a husband and his bride, but also to that of a mother for her children, a friend for a friend and a brother for his sibling. But of all human relationships, God's love is perhaps most often compared to the love of a good father for his children. For what does a good father do? He loves his children into existence and into maturity.

Many people have experienced bad fathers, but the God of the Bible is not like a bad father. He is not like a tyrant, a bully or a parent with impossible expectations, nor is he like a parent with no expectations – a parent who doesn't care or is never there. God is like a good father.

The Christian philosopher Peter Kreeft observes that God is often caricatured as a sort of benign, grandfatherly figure up in the clouds – sweet, kind and perhaps a bit doddery. But as he puts it:

God is not like a grandfather, he is like a father. Grandfathers are kind; fathers are loving. Grandfathers say, 'Run along and have a good time'; fathers say, 'But don't do this or that.' Grandfathers are compassionate, fathers are passionate.

In other words, a father's love is a committed love, a love committed to our best. A love that never gives up.

Perhaps the best illustration of this committed love is Jesus' parable of the Prodigal Son. It's the story of a man with two sons.

The younger son says to his father: 'I want you to give me my share of the family estate now.' Culturally, this was the ancient Hebrew equivalent of saying to his father: 'I wish you were dead.' However, the father doesn't get angry or disown his son. He grants his son's request. The younger son sells up his inheritance, leaves for a distant country and spends it all on wild living. Eventually broke and finding himself in the middle of a famine, he hires himself out to a farmer who assigns him the task of feeding pigs, which, for a young Jewish man, was really scraping the bottom of the barrel. Even worse, he is so hungry that he would gladly scrape the bottom of the barrel, in this case the pigs' feeding trough, just to put any sort of food in his mouth, but he wasn't permitted to do this. To the pig farmer, this young man's life was worth less than a pig's!

Then he remembers how workmen of his father were treated: well, and with food aplenty. So, he decides to return to his father in order to apologize for his behaviour and ask if his father will take him back as a hired servant. But, as the story goes, while he was still a long way off, his father saw him and was filled with compassion for him; he ran to his son, threw his arms around him and kissed him.

He ran to his son.

At the time, no self-respecting Middle-Eastern man would receive back a son who has treated him like this. But the father, who has been watching and waiting, publicly humiliates himself by running to the son and embracing him. Even before the son has a chance to give his apology speech, the father calls his servants to kill the prize calf and put on a big celebratory feast because his son 'was dead and is alive again, he was lost and is now found' (Luke 15.24, NIV).

But the story doesn't end yet.

The older son comes in from working the fields and is not one bit happy when he discovers that a party is going on to celebrate his younger brother's return. He is so furious that he insults his father in public with all the important people there by refusing to join in the celebration. With this insult fresh in everyone's mind, once more the father publicly humiliates himself, appearing weak, by going outside to plead with the older son to come inside to the party.

But the older son is angry, and he chastises the father for squandering a feast on someone who so clearly doesn't deserve it. He complains that never once did the father give him so much as a young goat to feast on and party with his friends, even though all these years he had been slaving away and never once broken a rule.

'My son,' the father says, 'you are always with me, and everything I have is yours. But we had to celebrate and be glad, because this brother of yours was dead and is alive again; he was lost and is found' (Luke 15.31—32, NIV). And so, the story ends.

Jesus told this now famous story to illustrate clearly for his Jewish listeners what God's love is really like. It's like the love of this father. A 'Never Stopping, Never Giving Up, Unbreaking, Always and Forever Love' of a father who longs to reconcile his estranged children to himself.

Both sons are rebels who neither respect their father nor want to live under his control. The younger takes what he can from the father with blatant disrespect. He is selfish and immoral. The older also takes what he can from the father, but with a grudging duty that makes him just as inwardly independent from the father as the son who runs away because in his mind he earns what he gets, he deserves it. That's why the elder brother was so angry that he refused to join the father's feast – from his perspective, the younger brother was getting what he didn't deserve.

In the end, who makes it to the feast with his father? The younger brother. And what was it that returned this prodigal's heart to his father? It wasn't the realization that he could get a better deal working for his dad as a labourer than working for the pig farmer. It was the father's loving embrace that eventually conquered his rebel heart, for, in the pigsty, he knew that he was dirty, but in the loving arms of his father, he understands just how deep the stain really is. In the pigsty, he felt sorry for himself but in the Father's arms, he feels sorry for his wickedness, for the way he has treated the one whose heart towards him contains only love.

As the theologian Karl Barth once wrote: 'Sin scorches us most after it comes under the scrutinizing light of God's forgiveness.' In the embrace of his father, the prodigal son's awareness of his wrongdoing was overwhelming, but so, too, was the awareness of his father's forgiveness and of his unfailing love for him. A love, like God's love, that breaks us and then puts us back together again, as we are meant to be.

But what about the elder brother? The father dearly loves his older son, too. He leaves the party to go outside to the son and invites him to join in the feast, explaining that everything that he has belongs to his older son as well, not because the son deserves it but because he is loved.

Will the elder brother be too proud to receive the love and forgiveness of the father from whom his heart is estranged? The story is left hanging with this question. But what we clearly see is that a loving relationship with the father is there for the taking. It is not something one earns by good behaviour or something from which one can be disqualified by bad behaviour. The most important question is a question of the heart. Does the elder son want the father? Does he love the father?

As the story ends there, the question is left hanging, not just for the elder son, but for every listener as well. Do we want to be with our heavenly Father? Do we want God in our lives or not? Whether we do or whether we don't, one thing from Jesus' story is clear: God wants to be with us because he loves us, unfailingly.

6

The matter of suffering

Where can I find hope in the midst of my pain?

Life is suffering

While writing this book, I read the BBC news page one morning, and here's a sample of the headlines for that day – a rising Coronavirus death toll; race-related hate crimes; massive job cuts across various industries; people scamming the vulnerable and elderly for money; rising homelessness; politicians calling each other names; fake news; fires destroying the Amazon rainforest. The sad thing was that I knew the news would be just as full of pain and suffering again the next day, and on all the days that followed.

Life hurts. There is so much pain in our world. So much evil. So much loss.

One response to life's suffering is to say, 'Well, I guess that's just the way things are,' and to try to be stoical or philosophical about it – to put on a stiff upper lip and just carry on as best as one can. But the problem is that even though a world full of suffering is just the way things are, we instinctively sense that the way things are is not the way things should be. Besides, just accepting suffering with a 'stiff upper lip' is easier said than done, particularly when you or someone you love are the ones in pain.

I remember sitting beside my grandmother's bed after she had been in an accident as a result of someone else's careless negligence. She took a horrible fall, shattering the bones in her legs and causing one of the main arteries in her leg to be pierced. She was taken to hospital, and we were told the pierced artery meant she would slowly bleed to death internally, over a number of days, and that, tragically, it was impossible for the doctors to operate. I sat by her side in those last couple of days as she was racked in pain, struggling to breathe and dying. If someone had said to me in that moment, 'Stiff upper lip, young fellow; that's just the way things are,' I would have punched them.

No matter how privileged your background, or charmed your existence, eventually life will bring you into first-hand contact with the central fact of suffering. The question then is how to respond to it, how to deal with it, how to live in the midst of the unavoidable reality of pain and loss.

We see this in the story of Prince Siddhartha Gautama, known to us today as the Buddha. As the story goes, the prince grew up in a palace knowing nothing about sickness or suffering or death. His parents purposely shielded him from these things by prohibiting the sick, the elderly and the suffering from entering the palace. Only when he was twenty-nine years old, did Prince Siddhartha finally venture out of the cocoon of the castle, accompanied by his servant Channa. When he came across an old man for the first time, he asked Channa what was wrong with the man. 'That is aging,' replied Channa. 'It happens to all of us.' The prince was shocked. Next, he saw a person suffering from a disease. 'What is wrong with him?' asked the prince. 'That is sickness and pain caused by disease,' replied Channa. 'We are all subject to it.' Again, the prince was stunned, having never seen illness or decay. Still reeling from these first two sights and the implications of what Channa had said, the prince saw a dead body. 'What is this?' asked the prince. 'It is death,' replied Channa. 'Eventually, it happens to all of us.'

Can you imagine just how shocking it must have been for the twenty-nine-year-old prince to encounter aging, sickness, pain and death for the first time in his life and to be told that they are an inevitable part of life? Can you imagine how alien they must have seen to him? How unnatural? How wrong? So unsettling and disturbing were these discoveries for Siddhartha Gautama that he left his palace, his family, wife and children, and devoted the rest of his life to finding a solution, or a way to deal with, what we might call the problem of suffering. He became the Buddha, and his eventual response to the question of suffering (one of the most influential answers in our world today), we shall consider in a moment, alongside others, including that of Christianity.

But unlike the experience of Prince Siddhartha (or the Buddha), the normal human experience is one of discovering the reality of sickness, suffering, ageing and death early on in life. From lost toys through to lost innocence, and from broken arms to broken homes, children soon discover that suffering and pain are as much a part of life as love and laughter. But even as children we sense that suffering and pain are somehow alien or wrong, in a way that love and laughter are not.

Why God, why?

The Bible affirms our instinct that the way the world is is not the way that it should be. It holds that something has gone terribly wrong with us and our world and that it has to do with our loss of connection with our Maker. Nonetheless, in my experience of talking to people about faith, the presence of evil and suffering in the world is probably the number one objection people raise against the existence of a creator God.

Influential atheists such as Stephen Fry or Sam Harris point to the litany of tragedies and misfortunes happening in our world today – from refugee crises, school shootings and suicide bombings to tsunamis, cancer and viruses – and ask: 'Where is this supposedly all-good, all-powerful God that Christians talk about? If he really cared about us, wouldn't he intervene? Wouldn't he do something about it? Doesn't life's cruel suffering make a mockery of all this religious babble about a God who loves us?'

However difficult this question is to face – and I have to say it is a very difficult question, indeed – it's actually a question that Christians think about, a lot. You even find the question echoed on numerous occasions in the Bible itself.

In John's Gospel, for example, we read a story about a man named Lazarus who is very sick. In fact, he is dying. Lazarus is a good friend of Jesus. He is the brother of Mary and Martha, who are also good friends of Jesus, so, naturally, the two sisters send word to Jesus: 'Lord, our brother Lazarus, the one you love, is very sick. Please come!' (John 11.3, TPT)

Jesus gets the message. But he doesn't leave straight away. He delays.

Meanwhile, the sisters sitting by Lazarus' side have to experience the horror of seeing Lazarus gradually overcome by a terrible sickness. Eventually, he dies. The natural question on everyone's lips was: 'Where was Jesus?' The message had been sent days ago, but Jesus didn't show up. Jesus didn't help.

When Jesus later makes it to Bethany, Lazarus has been dead a number of days. We read in the biblical account that:

> When Mary reached the place where Jesus was and saw him, she fell at his feet and said, 'Lord, if you had been here, my brother would not have died.'
> When Jesus saw her weeping, and the Jews who had come along with her also weeping, he was deeply moved in spirit and troubled. 'Where have you laid him?' he asked.
> 'Come and see, Lord,' they replied.
> Jesus wept.
> Then the Jews said, 'See how he loved him!'
> But some of them said, 'Could not he who opened the eyes of the blind man have kept this man from dying?'
> (John 11.32–37, NIV)

You see, the natural response of Mary and Martha and other friends and family was to ask: 'Lord, where were you? Why didn't you show up and do something? You have the power to stop this sort of thing. Why didn't you? Don't you even care?'

I wonder: have you ever asked God a question like that?

I have. The first time I did was sitting beside the hospital bed of my grandmother after her accident I mentioned earlier. As she was bleeding internally, her lungs slowly filled with fluid, and as each laboured breath got more difficult, I considered how it could be that an all-powerful God, who had the power to stop this, just didn't. 'Why not?' I wondered in frustration. 'Why is he allowing so much pain? Why, God? Why?'

We shouldn't be surprised if, like Mary and Martha, we find ourselves asking these sorts of questions in response to suffering. It is a very normal human reaction. And, what is Jesus' response to Mary? It is neither a response of anger at her questioning, nor is it a response of disinterest in her suffering.

In one of the most moving passages in the Bible, we read the words: 'Jesus wept.' If Jesus really is God, as Christians believe, it means that God in his divinity is not immune from our suffering. Whatever the reason for Jesus' failure to rescue his friends from suffering, his tears show that it is not indifference to their pain. In fact, in the book of Psalms, a book of poetry in the Bible, the Psalmist speaks of God as the one who holds all our tears in a bottle – a symbol that every moment of grief, loss and heartache we experience matters to God.

Nevertheless, suffering can still test one's belief in God's good-ness. Because, as human beings, we are tempted to think that if we were God, we would just get rid of suffering altogether. So, why doesn't God? That was the reaction of some of the onlookers in response to Jesus' late arrival to Lazarus' funeral: 'Could not he who opened the eyes of the blind man have kept this man from dying?'

Does suffering disprove God's existence?

The question of why God allows all this suffering if he is, in fact, good is as old as humanity. It is more than just a philosophical question. It is a cry of the heart, and for those in the midst of suffering, a philosophical response to the question is almost always unhelpful.

That being said, it is still an important philosophical question. For those who believe in the existence of a good God and who believe that this God makes sense of life, it is a question that must eventually be faced.

One of the first philosophers to articulate the question as a logical argument against God's existence was the ancient Greek philosopher, Epicurus. With great rhetorical force, he wrote:

Is God willing to prevent evil, but not able? Then He is not all-powerful. Is God able to prevent evil, but not willing? Then he is malevolent. Is He both able and willing? Then whence cometh evil? Is He neither able nor willing? Then why call him God?

More recently, the philosopher J. L. Mackie in his book entitled *The Miracle of Theism*, published in 1982, put the argument, known as 'the logical problem of evil', like this: 'If God is all-powerful and all-good, then he wouldn't allow suffering and evil. But suffering and evil exist. Therefore, an all-powerful, all-good God doesn't exist. Therefore, the God of the Bible doesn't exist.' Thus, Mackie argued that suffering logically disproves God's existence.

However, as we will see below, this argument can be refuted. Why? For the argument makes certain assumptions about suffering and about God that have been shown to be almost certainly false in philosophical circles.

But before considering the major philosophical defeater for the logical problem of evil, let me briefly note another observation many have made about suffering and our understanding of it in the West.

Is all suffering bad?

In the affluent West, we tend to view pain and suffering as our greatest enemies. We are accustomed to thinking about the ideal life in terms of unrestrained freedom, and of happiness in terms of the maximization of pleasure. Naturally, we tend to assume, therefore, that if God exists, he should create a world without pain or suffering.

In contrast, most non-Western cultures, throughout history, have regarded suffering not only as inevitable, but also as means of strengthening and enriching us. Such cultures see the meaning of life as something beyond this world and this life, whereas we tend to see this life as all there is. This makes it harder for us to face suffering or find any redeeming aspect to it.

A friend of mine grew up in Nepal, his parents medical missionaries who treated people with leprosy. He explained to me that leprosy is caused by a bacterium that destroys nerve endings so that a person loses the ability to feel pain. It's not the leprosy that causes deformity in hands and feet, it's the persistent injuries that occur as a result of the person being unable to experience pain and suffering. They stub their toe or put their hand in the fire and don't realize it. It gave me pause to reflect on the nature of pain, and I realized that, until then, I had always thought of pain as something entirely negative. But as my friend's story indicated, that's clearly not the case. Pain can be helpful. And, as all psychologists worth their salt will attest, pain and suffering can help us grow as human beings. They help us, for example, to develop patience, as well as compassion and understanding towards others. I've heard it said that the best doctors for treating an illness are those who have had to go through the pain and suffering of that illness themselves because they understand exactly what their patients are going through.

Isn't it interesting that although we see suffering as inherently bad, we are much more likely to admire and trust the person who has come through the other side of pain and adversity, than we are a person for whom everything has always come easily? The writer John Eldredge once said: 'I don't trust a man who hasn't suffered.' A statement like this points to a deep truth – that suffering helps to develop our character, whereas a pain-free life tends to stunt it.

And for some reason, suffering often causes people to live at a much deeper, more purposeful level than they did before suffering. In an influential article, published in the *New York Times* in 2014 and entitled 'What suffering does', the journalist David Brooks wrote:

> People who suffer often feel an overwhelming moral responsi-
> bility to respond well to it. They don't say, 'Well, I'm feeling a
> lot of pain over the loss of my child. I should try to balance my
> pleasure account by going to a lot of parties and living it up.'
> No. Parents who've lost a child start foundations. Prisoners
> in the concentration camp with psychologist Viktor Frankl
> rededicated themselves to living up to the hopes and expecta-
> tions of their loved ones, even though those loved ones might
> themselves already be dead.

Experience teaches us that suffering often causes people to live less selfish and more meaningful lives. Something else suffering often does is cause people to consider God's existence seriously, often for the first time. The French philosopher Luc Ferry, in his bestselling book, *A Brief History of Thought*, observes that it is our experiences of heartbreak, tragedy and suffering, more than anything else in this life, that incline us to consider whether in fact there is more to life than this life.

Lewis echoes this idea when he writes: 'God whispers to us in our pleasures, speaks in our consciences, but shouts in our pain. It is his megaphone to rouse a deaf world.' Suffering, in a way, forces us to think about what life is really all about. As much as it causes many to question the existence of a loving God, it is just as true that it causes many, who have never given God a second thought, to do so – and maybe even to turn to him for help.

Suffering, love and freedom

We see then that the question of suffering is complex, and that it is simplistic to assume that all suffering is necessarily bad or devoid of any purpose. However, the primary objection to the argument that suffering logically disproves God's existence is an objection based not on the value of suffering per se, but on the importance of love and of freedom. It is known as the 'free-will defence', and most notably put forward by philosophers such as Alvin Plantinga. It goes something like this:

If God is good, he would want to create the best of all possible worlds. And the best of all possible worlds is arguably a world that allows for love, for love is arguably the highest of all goods. But in order to create a world that allows for love, it must be a world full of creatures who have the ability to love. And in order for creatures to have the ability to love they must be given genuine moral freedom (that is, a free will); because love that is not freely given is not truly love. Yet, for creatures to possess genuine moral freedom means that those creatures must also be granted the freedom to choose to reject God and his love: to choose to live selfishly rather than lovingly. Certainly, God could create a world without any evil and suffering by instead creating 'automatons' (creatures without free will who always do the right thing like pre-programmed robots), but then such a world would allow no space for love. Thus, the best of all possible worlds is arguably a world that, in allowing for the possibility of love, must also allow for the reality of freedom, and therefore the possibility of pain.

If this argument is correct, it means the presence of evil and suffering in our world is best understood, not as a sign of God's lack of love but of his commitment to love, knowing full well the risks that this commitment brings with it. Love, it might be said, risks suffering. Ask any parent, and they will tell you that's true!

Interestingly, the biblical story of creation confirms this philosophical line of reasoning, holding that when God chose to create, he didn't choose automatons to populate his world, he chose us. Creatures with the freedom to choose. Creatures with the freedom to love. It also teaches that the life and freedom God gave us, to choose love, we have used to reject God's love and wisdom, and that our relationships have fractured as a result – not only our relationships with God and with others, but also with ourselves and even with nature. Christianity maintains that we are broken – morally, relationally and spiritually broken – and that we see the evidence of this brokenness in our lives (and in our newspapers) every day.

The uniqueness of the Christian response

But if the world is broken, while God is good, wouldn't we expect him to do something, rather than simply watch all that is going on from a distance, leaving us to our brokenness and mess? According to the Bible, he has done something: in Jesus Christ, God himself entered into our world of suffering, in human flesh, to rescue us. In doing so, he has experienced what it is like to suffer – to be hungry, cold and tired; misunderstood, betrayed and rejected; humiliated, tortured and killed.

Of all the major responses to suffering, this is absolutely unique. We see this most clearly when we consider the Bible's response to the question of suffering against the alternative responses available.

Consider, first, the karmic response to suffering. Put simply, this is the idea that if you do good things, good things will happen to you; and if you do bad things, bad things will happen to you. We see this sort of thinking at work in the Hindu caste system, for example. If you are born into the high Brahmin caste of priests and teachers, it is held to be because of the good you did in your previous lives, whereas if you are born into the lowest of the low, the Dalit caste where people are viewed as 'untouchables', then the poverty, alienation and shame you experience is held to be because of the wrongs you did in your past lives. In short, Karma holds that the cause or reason behind all the bad things that have happened to you is you and all the bad things you have done.

In contrast, the Buddha rejected the idea of the Hindu caste system that was prevalent in his society. Buddha himself came to the conclusion that suffering is ultimately an illusion, caused by a false attachment to, or desire for, the particulars of this world – be it fame, possessions, relationships or something else. To avoid suffering, he taught, one must cease desiring things. One must detach oneself entirely from the things in this world. Detachment comes from realizing that everything is One and One is everything; and that because there are no particulars in life, but only Oneness, there are in fact no desirables to desire, nor possessions to possess, nor relations to relate with. Like a single drop of water which dissolves in the ocean, we achieve true enlightenment, he taught, when we let go of our desires and even our identity and dissolve into the universal Oneness of everything. And, as some have pointed out, Buddha himself lived up to this principle of detachment when he left his palace and family, on the day his son was born, to fulfil his quest for personal enlightenment.

According to another major system of belief, Islam, there is one God, Allah, and he controls everything, including the actions of every individual. Thus, for mainstream Islam, human beings do not have any free will. God has already foreordained everything in advance. Since everything that happens is God's will and since suffering happens, suffering is God's will. And because suffering is God's will, our only response can be to submit to it. We must not question suffering, we must endure it, and it is our ability to submit to suffering rather than question it, which allows Allah to see who is and who is not truly righteous upon the face of the earth.

Now, if you are an atheist, you might regard all these attempts to understand and make sense of suffering as nothing more than misguided religious attempts that refuse to face reality. What reality? Well, from the perspective of the atheist Dawkins, the reality that there is no supernatural element to life, be it God, Karma or whatever else one might appeal to in order to make sense of suffering.

According to Dawkins, suffering is not just or unjust, right or wrong, it's just bad luck. After all, as he says in his book, *River Out of Eden*:

> In a universe of blind physical forces and genetic replication, some people are going to get hurt, other people are going to get lucky, and you won't find any rhyme or reason in it, nor any justice. The universe we observe has precisely the properties we should expect if there is, at bottom, no design, no purpose, no evil, and no good, nothing but blind, pitiless indifference.

In other words, lion eats zebra, wolf eats lamb, strong hurts weak and that's just the way it is. Some atheist philosophers (though not all atheist philosophers, it must be said) have even suggested that this is not only the way things are, it is also the way things ought to be – including in human relationships. The atheist, Nietzsche, for example, taught that the strong should dominate the weak, and suffering is nature's way of weeding out the weak and helping us to evolve. You might think such crazy ideas could exist solely in the ivory towers of academic speculation, but you need only study the former concentration camps of Auschwitz or Birkenau to see how the dangerous ideologies of yesterday's philosophers sometimes become the guiding principles of tomorrow's powers that be. Though few realize this, Adolph Hitler was actually very much influenced by Nietzsche and his philosophical ideas.

So you can see that, when it comes to the question of suffering, there are some very different explanations on offer and the differences really make a difference.

For example, in contrast to some other responses to suffering, Christianity doesn't assume that suffering is deserved, so we should do nothing about it. It doesn't say that suffering is just an illusion, so we should ignore it. It doesn't say that suffering is just God's will, so we shouldn't question it. And it doesn't say that suffering is just natural, so we should accept it. It neither denies nor diminishes the reality of evil and suffering. In fact, Christianity confirms the cry of our hearts – that the way this suffering world is, is not the way that it should be.

And in response to a suffering world, it offers a suffering saviour. Jesus Christ.

A reason to trust

None of this means that Christians are somehow immune to the realities of suffering, or that Christians have quick and easy answers to life's tragedies; or that suffering doesn't cause Christians to ask hard questions of God. As we see throughout the Bible, prophets, poets and ordinary people are given scope to vent their frustration and agony towards God in the midst of evil and suffering. We see this, particularly, in the book of Psalms; and we see that God doesn't smite his people for their anger and tears. As we have noted,

Jesus himself wept in response to the suffering of death, even as he had come into the world to defeat it. The God of the Bible acknowledges our suffering and is moved by it.

Nicholas Wolterstorff, a philosopher from Yale University and a Christian, wrote a book about the death of his son Eric called *Lament for a Son*. Once asked in an interview why he wrote the book, he responded:

> My little book *Lament for a Son* is not a book about grief. It is a cry of grief. After the death of our son, I dipped into a number of books about grief. I could not read them. It was impossible for me to reflect on grief in the abstract. I was in grief. My book is a grieving cry. In the course of my cry I hold out the vision of God as with me in my grief, of God as grieving with me; God with me in my mourning.

He goes on to say the most difficult question about suffering is: 'Why does God permit moral evil and suffering that serves no discernible good?' He explains:

> If we believe that God suffers in response to our suffering, then in addition to that question we have another: why does God allow what God endures in tears? I do not know the answer. In faith I live the question.

In other words, when it comes to the question of suffering, Christians have some good answers – both comprehensive and nuanced – but they do not profess to have all the answers. The Bible explains why there is suffering in the world, generally speaking (we have already talked about how a world that allows for love must also be a world that allows for suffering, and how not all suffering is purposeless). But at the same time, the Bible does not give Christians warrant to speak to each and every particular instance of suffering and say: 'I know why God has allowed that particular accident, disease or tragedy to occur.'

When tragedies strike, one thing Christianity doesn't offer is simplistic answers. It certainly resists the karmic perspective which assumes the one who suffers must have done something bad. When asked by his followers about the fall of a tower in Siloam in which a number of people were killed, Jesus is clear that the victims of this tragedy weren't necessarily worse people than anyone else who wasn't killed. He acknowledges that tragedies happen to the just and to the unjust, to the kind and the unkind, and that that's part of the mystery of life, this side of heaven.

In the book of Job, one of the wisdom books of the Bible, we find the notion that, as human beings, we aren't always given the reasons behind everything that happens to us. When Job suffers immense pain and loss in his life, he cries out to God in his pain and confusion for an answer to why this is happening. Job's friends assume Job must somehow secretly deserve the suffering he is experiencing, otherwise God wouldn't allow it to happen. But we, the readers, know this is clearly not the case. And God rebukes Job's friends for the simplistic way in which they assume Job must have been in the wrong simply because he is suffering. However, when God does speak to Job at the end of the book, he doesn't give Job the answers he has been looking for. He doesn't reveal to Job why he has allowed Job to suffer the way he has. He simply reminds Job of who he (God) is and who he (Job) is. His answer to Job (in chapter 38) goes something like this: 'Job, were you there when I laid the earth's foundation? Did you set the limits of the sea? Did you bring forth the stars in their constellations?' In meeting God, Job realizes how little he comprehends or even could comprehend of the big cosmic picture that God oversees. Job glimpses the majesty of God's sovereignty, and in the end, it is enough for Job. He falls to his knees. God himself is the answer.

I remember the first time I took my then eighteen-month-old daughter Grace to be vaccinated. My wife said she would find it too difficult to watch the whole thing happen (it really isn't pleasant seeing someone stick a giant needle into your child's arm), so she graciously 'volunteered' me for the job. I remember feeling really nervous about how Grace would react to the needle and what she would think of me, her loving father, when she saw that I had allowed her to be hurt. You see, your job as the parent is to sit your child on your lap and make him or her feel as relaxed and comfortable as possible with what is going on, so the nurse can safely stick the needle in. In other words, they make you entirely complicit with the act.

So, as my daughter was happily sitting on my lap, smiling at me and at the nurse with the pretty and shiny pointy object in her hand, I braced myself for what I knew would be a shock to Grace. And as that needle went in, and Grace's face instantly went red, shifting from an expression of contentment to one of shock and pain, I kept my eyes on her eyes, afraid I would read in her face the fear that somehow, I, who was allowing this to happen, no longer loved her. But thankfully, I never saw that look. What I did see in the expression of her now tear-stained face was the question, 'Why?' 'Why, Daddy? Given that I know you love me, why are you allowing this to happen?'

The reality was that Grace was of an age such that even if I had tried to explain it to her, she wouldn't have understood. But the fact that an eighteen-month old didn't have the capacity to understand why any good parent would allow a stranger to stick a painful needle into her arm didn't mean that there were no good reasons. I knew that one day she would possess the capacity to understand, but that for now all she had to go on was her trust in me. But her trust was not an unreasonable trust. It was not a blind faith. It was a faith in me based on the evidence of my love for her from the very first day of her life.

Similarly, Christianity holds that we can trust God has good reasons for allowing to happen what he does in this life, even if we ourselves can't understand those reasons; that he is wise, and he is good and that one day we will understand. But not today, and in all likelihood, not in this lifetime. Someone may object and say that this is just blind faith. But according to the Bible, it's not. It is a faith based on evidence. What evidence? Well, pre-eminently, the life, death and resurrection of the person, Jesus Christ. The one who the Bible says loved us and gave himself for us.

As the Russian novelist Dostoevsky stared at Hans Holbein the Younger's painting *Dead Christ in the Tomb*, he was struck by this profound truth – that no other God has scars. He saw that the cross is God's answer to a hurting world. As New York pastor, Tim Keller, writes: 'We may not know the exact reason why we suffer in any given instance, but one thing our suffering cannot mean. In light of the cross it cannot mean that God doesn't love us.'

In other words, followers of Jesus believe that even though they don't know everything, they can have faith in the one who does. Not only, as the book of Job explains, because his ways are higher than our ways, but also, as Christ's scars demonstrate, because God is not aloof from our suffering. He, too, knows what it is like to suffer.

A reason for hope

Christians understand that just as the cross reminds us that this world is not the way it should be, so too, the resurrection assures us that this world will one day be restored to what it should be. The resurrection is a foretaste of the truth that this life of suffering and death is not all there is. That there is hope and meaning beyond this world and life: beyond it but not separate from it – for this life is but part of a story, and the final chapter hasn't happened yet.

It's like Mary, the sister of Lazarus, in the Bible story I mentioned earlier, weeping at the feet of Jesus because Lazarus is now dead, and wondering why Jesus was not there to save him. But as those familiar with Lazarus' story know, this is not the end of the story.

For, in the midst of a grieving community, when all hope seems lost, Jesus finally walks to the tomb of Lazarus and cries out in a loud voice: 'Lazarus, come out.' And to the wonderment of all, Lazarus, now raised to life, does exactly that. And in the blink of an eye – tears of sadness are transformed into tears of utter joy.

Christians hold on to the hope, in the midst of suffering and grief, that this is not the end of the story. That, one day, Jesus will wipe away every tear from every eye. That one day, the sting of suffering will be removed. That one day, all that is wrong will be put right. And that one day, in the words of Samwise Gamgee from *The Lord of the Rings*, all that is sad in the world will come untrue.

And in the meantime? As Christian writer Henrietta C. Mears writes: 'I know not the way he leads me, but well do I know my guide.' In other words, Christians put their ultimate hope not in the guarantee of a pain-free life in which everything makes sense, but in the person of Jesus Christ. Not only because, as they see it, where else better would they have to go? But also because they consider that Jesus is worthy of their trust and that he has the scars to prove it.

I will be with you

When dark times of suffering come, as they inevitably will, the human heart instinctively cries out, 'why?' This is what we do. It is part of what it means to be human. But have you ever wondered, with regard to those who do not believe in a God, to whom this 'why' is being addressed?

Lewis, whose Narnia series has brought so much joy to young readers, himself suffered a sad childhood. He tragically lost his mother at a very young age and his father provided very little emotional support. As a result, he lost whatever faith he had in a loving God. Lewis describes himself as a young man, before he turned back to faith, as living in a whirl of contradictions. He writes: 'I maintained that God did not exist. I was also very angry with God for not existing. And I was equally angry with God for creating such a world as this.'

Lewis discovered that suffering does not get easier when we get rid of God and that the solace offered by even the best of philosophy, literature or poetry – all of which he was well-acquainted with – cannot offer what the Christian faith he had rejected offered – that is, a friend who loves us and who truly understands what we are going through. A friend who is completely for us. And a friend who promises to be with us, even through life's darkest valleys, including the valley of the shadow of death. A friend, that is, in God.

The Bible teaches that the problem of suffering is one that God takes seriously. Our pain matters to him, and he himself knows what it is like to suffer. But according to the God of the Bible, our greatest problem, more serious even than our suffering, is our separation from him. God does not promise us a life free of suffering, but he does promise to be with us, in our suffering, if we want him to be there.

We see that when God's people in the Bible are about to go through a challenging time, God often encourages them with a certain phrase. The phrase begins with 'Fear not'. But he doesn't say: 'Fear not, for I have promised you a pain-free life.' He says: 'Fear not, for I will be *with* you.' Christian faith, while offering no quick and easy answers to the profound question of suffering, speaks meaningfully to the question; and, for the one who is suffering, these five words, 'I will be with you', can make all the difference in the world.

Part 2

EXAMINING THE EVIDENCE

7

Thinking faith
When does belief make sense?

In the first half of this book, I tried to show how Christianity speaks to the things in life that really matter – things like meaning, significance, goodness, truth, love and hope in the midst of suffering. I have pointed out that Christianity explains why these things affect and matter to us and that we also find in Jesus an answer to and fulfilment of the things that matter to us. In other words, I have tried to show how Christianity, or more to the point, Christ himself, not only explains the longings of the human heart, but also how he is their ultimate satisfaction as well.

Now, in the second half of this book, I wish to explore the question: but how can we know this is all true?

When something sounds very good, we instinctively feel it may be too good to be true. There is always the fear of falling victim to the impressive sales pitch, of being led by our emotions to buy into something that wasn't all that it was cracked up to be – like the fine-looking house, the price of which seemed too good to be true, that we later discover has major problems with its foundations.

No sensible person buys a house without carrying out a full inspection of the property. Likewise, we shouldn't commit ourselves to any major decision in life without some careful thinking. That's why we shall consider together, in the second part of this book, the important questions of reason and evidence. Is it reasonable to believe that the Christian description of life, the universe and everything is true? It may sound good or attractive or beautiful . . . but is it real? Is it solid? Does it stand up to rigorous scrutiny and careful investigation?

Proof and certainty

As a lawyer, I have sometimes been asked whether the case for Christianity is solid enough to withstand the sort of scrutiny that a lawyer would bring to bear in assessing the strength of a case brought before him or her. When I tell people that I think that it is, that actually there is a very compelling case for Christianity, the reply is almost always: 'Ok then. Show me the proof! Lawyers are meant to be interested in proof. What's the proof for Christianity?' And this is the answer I tend to give: 'Well, it depends on what you mean by proof!'

For example, it can be 'proven', deductively, that $1 + 1 = 2$; however, this type of proof doesn't exist outside of the realm of pure mathematics. But you and I live in the real world, as do lawyers or judges, who must often make important decisions regarding cases brought before them in the real world. In contrast to mathematical proof, proof from a legal perspective simply means establishing a fact by means of evidence.

While we should not expect that Christianity can be demonstrated to be true in the same way that one would prove a mathematical equation – for real life is not like that – it is nonetheless reasonable to expect that, if Christianity were true, one could point to a substantial amount of evidence in support of it, much like a lawyer in a court of law would do in presenting his or her case. The remaining chapters of this book are meant to serve as an introduction to that evidence.

With respect to evidence, I sometimes find myself in conversation with people who say that they will only believe in God if God's existence can be demonstrated scientifically, by which they usually mean, when pressed, in a laboratory. But then, how many of our beliefs would pass this test? For example, we learn at school that Julius Caesar invaded England about 2,000 years ago, even though nobody can demonstrate this fact in a science laboratory. Does that mean we should throw away all our history books for lack of proof?

Of course not. Like our legal system, history is a discipline that weighs and considers evidence. In this case, historical evidence. And based on the historical evidence, belief in the invasion of Britain by Julius Caesar is a most reasonable and sensible belief.

Though Christianity cannot be demonstrated to be true in a science lab, it is nevertheless a most reasonable and sensible faith in light of the evidence that supports it. And, by the way, some of that evidence includes historical evidence because Christianity makes claims about things that God has done in history.

Moreover, even though the truth of Christianity cannot be proven in a science lab, some of the evidence in support of it comes from science, which sometimes surprises people – especially those who feel that science could never support the existence of something we cannot see. However, this stems from a misunderstanding. As Oxford Professor Alister McGrath points out, science itself often proposes the existence of things that cannot be seen or observed – such as dark matter – to explain things that can be seen or observed. The Higgs boson particle (a sub-atomic particle whose existence physicists predicted in the 1960s but which was not observed until 2012) is a great example of something that scientists believed existed even though they couldn't physically observe it. The reason why they believed it existed, even though they could not observe it, was that its existence made sense of everything else that they could observe at the sub-atomic level.

It was on the basis of a very similar process of reasoning that the German High Command during the Second World War correctly concluded that their 'unbreakable' enigma code had in fact been broken by the English. Although they had no direct observable evidence of their code being broken, it was far and away the best explanation of why the English were so regularly able to intercept German troops. And although it was difficult to believe their 'unbreakable' code had been broken, it was even more difficult to believe that all these English intercepts could be happening solely by chance.

Similarly, one of the reasons why belief in a God, who cannot be seen (at least for now), makes rational sense is that God's existence makes so much sense of everything else that we can see. This is one of the reasons why I became a Christian. As I considered the various explanations on offer for the existence of life, the universe and everything, it seemed to me that the Christian understanding of reality had the most power to explain why it is that the universe is precisely the way it is, and why it is that we as human beings are precisely the way that we are.

Worldview on trial

Christianity, at heart, is about a relationship with God. But it is also a comprehensive worldview. A worldview is a conception we hold about the basic constitution of reality, affecting, at the most fundamental level, how we approach life in this world. Or to put it another way, our worldview is like a lens through which we view and interpret our world, influencing the way we see ourselves, other people and the environment around us. It consists of our most foundational assumptions about life, the universe and everything.

And whether we are consciously aware of it or not, all of us have a worldview because we all have beliefs about reality. If I wanted to understand your worldview, for example, these four big questions could provide me with insight. First, where did life come from? Second, what is the meaning of life? Third, how should one live in this world? And finally, what happens to us when we die?

There are many different worldviews on offer. Some are religious and some not. No matter your background, I would suggest that if you want to better understand the world you live in, including your fellow human beings who inhabit this world, it helps if you develop a basic understanding of the major worldviews that people commonly possess.

If you are going to do this, it helps to know, as you begin your investigations, that most of the major worldviews on offer fall into one of three broad categories – (1) atheistic naturalism, (2) pantheism and (3) theism. Atheistic naturalism is the view that a purely physical universe is the ultimate reality: there is no supernatural or divine dimension to existence. Pantheism is the view that everything is ultimately undifferentiated Oneness, and that that Oneness is divine. Theism is the view that there is a personal God who created this physical universe.

Christianity, Islam and Judaism are all monotheistic in that they all believe in one creator God. Philosophical Hinduism and Classical Buddhism are both pantheistic. They both believe, ultimately, in a divine oneness. Secular humanism and existentialism both align with atheistic naturalism. They both reject any spiritual dimension to reality.

Clearly, Christianity is not the only worldview on offer – nor, so to speak, is it the only worldview on trial. In a sense, all worldviews are called to give an account of why it is that they best explain and make sense of this extraordinary world in which we happen to find ourselves. All worldviews are called to give an account of the evidence – in this case, the evidence being all of observed reality – whether that includes data from history, philosophy, science, psychology or from personal experience.

One of the major reasons that the brilliant Lewis became a Christian was because he believed that Christianity made such remarkable sense of all of observed reality. As he famously said: 'I believe in Christianity as I believe that the sun has risen: not only because I see it, but because by it I see everything else.'

My own experience of coming to believe that Christianity is true was similar. As I observed this marvellous and complex universe and thought about all the major explanations for its existence, Christianity seemed to me the only worldview that, like the right key, exactly fitted the lock, and in doing so unlocked the meaning behind it all.

Of course, this is something that all must freely investigate for themselves and come to their own conclusion about. It is not something that should be forced on anyone. Indeed, from where I sit as a Christian, Christianity is not something that can be forced on anyone because, even though it is a worldview, it is first and foremost a loving relationship with God. And love must be freely given in order to be truly love.

When it comes to the question of what is most fundamentally true about life, the universe and everything, each person must think, investigate and weigh up the evidence for themselves. What evidence? Well, the evidence of the amazingly complex and wonderful world around us, as well as that of the amazingly complex and wonderful world within us.

8

The evidence around us
Here by accident or on purpose?

Have you ever experienced a sense of wonder and awe when looking at the natural world? The exquisite beauty of the cosmos, the kaleidoscope colours of a coral reef, the serenity of a sunset, the grandeur of a majestic mountain range, the awesome power of a great waterfall or the incredible intricacy of the human body and the way its different systems work together? The great twentieth-century scientist Albert Einstein observed: 'He to whom this emotion is a stranger, who can no longer pause to wonder and stand rapt in awe, is as good as dead: his eyes are closed.'

The Bible teaches us that the awe and wonder we experience in response to what really is an amazing world around us should naturally lead our minds to the person who made this world – in the same way, the artist is evident in great art or a designer in great design.

The famous Jewish king and poet, David, writes: 'The heavens declare the glory of God; the skies proclaim the work of his hands. Day after day they pour forth speech; night after night they reveal knowledge' (Psalms 19.1–2, NIV). David was firmly of the view that the world around us doesn't explain itself. That it somehow points beyond itself, to a creator.

But sometimes you'll hear sceptics suggesting that science – which studies the natural world around us – has somehow disproved or done away with the need for God, such that a person continuing to believe in God in the twenty-first century is like an adult still believing in Santa Claus or the tooth fairy long after his or her childhood.

I remember being at university studying law and a friend's older brother, who was doing his PhD in biology, telling me confidently that science had certainly disproved God. As a non-scientist, I had no idea how to respond, for he evidently knew more about science than I did. And it really caused me to question whether belief in God was truly rational.

Science and God: friends or foes?

But actually, the more I read about the relationship between science and belief in God, the more I realized that science and belief in God have been friends right from the very beginning and still are today.

What do I mean by that? Well, one of the wonderful things about working in the city of Oxford is getting to meet a lot of clever people. Many of those clever people are scientists, and many of those clever scientists are Christians. Which raises an obvious question: how can science and faith be in conflict when at the University of Oxford, one of the leading universities in the world, you will find people who believe in God, go to church and are also world-class scientists?

Actually, and this is something few people are aware of, many of the world's leading scientists are Christians. People such as Francis Collins (former Head of the Human Genome Project and current Head of the National Institutes of Health), Don Page (the renowned theoretical physicist who studied under Stephen Hawking), Rosalind Picard (Professor of Media Arts and Sciences at Massachusetts Institute of Technology), Richard Smalley (a Nobel Prize winner in chemistry), Charles H. Townes (a Nobel Prize winner in physics), Werner Arber (a Nobel Prize winner in medicine), John Gurdon (a Nobel Prize winner in developmental biology), Joseph Murray (a Nobel Prize winner in physiology, who pioneered the concept of transplant surgery), Raymond Vahan Damadian (inventor of the magnetic resonance imagining (MRI) machine), Simon C. Morris Lyall (medal winner for contributions to earth science) and Allan Sandage (until his death, the world's greatest living astronomer).

This is not surprising when one considers that it was actually belief in God that provided the theoretical foundations for the beginnings of modern science. Copernicus, Galileo, Kepler, Newton, Boyle and Pascal all believed that God had created an ordered universe whose laws, because they were ordered, could be discovered. And so, for them, it made sense to try to discover these laws. The universe, they reasoned, must be intelligible because behind it all, they believed, was an intelligence.

Clearly then, the narrative that there is a conflict between science and belief in God is wrong. So why do people think there must be a conflict? The reason is because there is one – but it is not between science and belief in God. The real conflict is between two competing belief systems – between belief in God (theism) and belief that there is no God (atheism).

Science itself is actually neutral. As long as you believe in a material universe you can do science, and, of course, Christians do believe in a material universe, as do atheists. That is why both theists and atheists can do great science. Where they differ is, Christians believe that God created the material universe we study, whereas many atheists believe this material universe is all there is.

Science is great, but it's also limited

The other thing to bear in mind is that science, as wonderful as it truly is, nevertheless cannot answer all the important questions of life. Don't get me wrong, I think science is great, but it has its limitations. Which is why, at a university, science is not the only faculty of knowledge – there are also history, philosophy and theology, among others.

One of the reasons people think science has done away with belief in God is because they are convinced that science now answers all the questions that religion previously addressed, thereby making God redundant. The classic illustration of this is that when primitive people heard thunder, they believed it must be the gods beating their drums; or in Norse tradition, that it was Chris Hemsworth, I mean Thor, the god of thunder, striking his hammer. However, now that we are modern science-embracing people, we know the real cause of thunder. So, we no longer need to cling to any primitive superstitious beliefs about God.

However, to believe that our increased scientific knowledge means we have done away with or disproved God is to show a fundamental misunderstanding of the nature of both science and of belief in God, at least of the Judeo-Christian variety.

Let me put it like this: if you had the technical skill set to pull apart an Apple iPhone and eventually figured out how all the different components of that phone worked, would you have thereby disproved the existence of Steve Jobs, the creator of the iPhone? Of course not. Just because you are able to figure out what everything is and how it works doesn't mean that there is no designer. Likewise, even if scientists were to figure out, one day, how all the different parts of the material universe work, science would neither have proved nor disproved a designer God behind it all.

You see, science is very good at answering the 'how' and the 'what' questions of the universe but not the 'why'. Why is this universe here? Why are we here? Such questions lie outside the field of science. That doesn't mean that when it comes to understanding things, science is not a good thing. It just means that when it comes to understanding things, science is not everything. Science is great. But it's also limited.

How science points to God

Although science, by its nature, can neither prove nor disprove the existence of God, it does provide us with clues, and those clues point strongly towards the existence of a creator.

Throughout human history, many great thinkers, both ancient and modern, have spoken of how the universe gives this overwhelming impression of order and design, from which it is rational to infer an 'orderer' or creator behind it all.

Take something as simple as the human hand, for example. When you look at a hand, the overwhelming impression is that it is ordered and designed for specific purposes which are intelligible or recognizable to the intelligent mind. We observe in the hand dexterity and sensitivity for touching: just perfect for the recognizable purposes of grasping, moving and manipulating things.

The same teleological (purposeful) quality in life which we see at the anatomical level, we also see at the microscopic level and the astronomical level. As British astrophysicist Paul Davies has noted: 'The impression of design in the universe is overwhelming.'

Indeed, up until the nineteenth century, most of the great thinkers believed this overwhelming impression of order and design made it rational to infer the existence of a designer God. After all, if there is no God why would the universe be ordered and intelligible? Why wouldn't it be chaotic?

William Paley's famous watchmaker analogy was highly influential in promoting belief in a designer God. In his work entitled *Natural Theology* (1802), Paley amassed a catalogue of examples from the field of natural sciences of various compelling evidences of design in the natural world. His most memorable example was the human eye, which Paley was able to show represented a finely tuned mechanism of irreducible complexity. Move or remove just one of the parts – the lens, the retina, the cornea or any other – and we wouldn't be able to see anything.

Using examples such as this, Paley introduced his famous watchmaker analogy. He argued that if, not knowing what a watch was, we happened to stumble upon one on the ground one day, we wouldn't conclude that natural causes had produced this thing because of the incredible intricacy, order, design and irreducible

117

complexity that we would observe in it. In the same way, he argued, remarkable biological mechanisms, like the human eye, should lead us to conclude that an intelligent mind must be behind it all.

Because of arguments like these, most thinking people believed there must be an intelligent cause or creator behind the world. That was, at least, until the publication of Charles Darwin's *Origin of the Species* in 1859 and his theory of evolution. What Darwin did in effect was to say: 'You don't need an intelligent designer to explain how complex biological things like plants and animals (including eyes) could exist because they can be explained entirely by natural processes such as natural selection and mutation operating over long periods of time, in accordance with natural laws.' Darwin himself wrote:

> The old argument of design in nature, as given by Paley, which formerly seemed to me so conclusive, fails, now that the law of natural selection has been discovered. We can no longer argue that, for instance, the beautiful hinge of a bivalve shell must have been made by an intelligent being, like the hinge of a door by man. There seems to be no more design in the variability of organic beings and in the action of natural selection, than in the course which the wind blows. Everything in nature is the result of fixed laws.

It's mostly because of the influence of Darwin's theory of evolution that many laypeople now believe that science has done away with the need for God. When, in fact, all Darwin actually did was provide us with a theory about how we could move from simple forms of biological life, like the humble bacterium, to complex forms of biological life, like you and me (of course, some of us are more complex than others!). But his theory does not explain, or even attempt to explain, the far more fundamental questions of how life could even begin in the first place, and how it is that we live in a universe capable of sustaining that life.

When we consider those fundamental questions – where life and this life-permitting universe come from – we find the scientific data providing us with powerful evidence or clues pointing not away from but towards the existence of a grand designer behind it all.

So, let's have a look at these clues. The first clue is so big and so obvious that it is easy for it to be, as they say, hidden in plain sight. For the first clue is the existence of the universe itself.

Clue 1: the existence of the universe

One of the most fundamental questions is this: why is there something rather than nothing? There didn't have to be a material universe, but there is. How did this universe get here?

Philosophers tell us that there are only three possible explanations for the existence of the universe. The first explanation is that the universe has just always existed: it is eternal. The second explanation is that the universe popped into existence by itself: it is self-generated. The third explanation is that God brought the universe into existence: it is created.

But as of the last fifty years, we know, at least if we are interested in modern physics, that the universe had a beginning. That's the overwhelming consensus view. And unless we are willing to dismiss scientific consensus on the matter, we must remove the first explanation – that the universe is eternal – from the table of options. This then leaves us with two remaining alternatives. Either the universe is self-generated, or God brought it into existence, which means it is created.

Science also tells us that nothing physical exists without a cause. For example, the clouds in the sky are physical. They have a cause. You also are physical. So, you have a cause. If you do not know your cause, you may want to speak to your parents. This universe is also physical; therefore, it, too, must have had a cause. But if the universe

119

had a cause, this rules out the second explanation: that the universe just popped into existence, by itself, without any cause.

That leaves us then with only one remaining explanation for the cause of the universe: God (sometimes referred to by philosophers as the 'first cause' or 'unmoved mover').

Some people might respond by saying: 'Well, then who created God?' And I can see why they would think it. It's because we live in a physical universe in which we are used to everything having a cause. We assume therefore that God should also have a cause. But unlike this universe, God is not physical. God, by definition, is spirit or unbodily personal power. There is therefore is no logical or scientific reason why God should have a cause.

Thus, of the three possible explanations, the only one we have no reason to rule out on grounds of reason or science is the third one – that God created the universe. Now, the idea that God created the universe might sound fantastical to some; however, from a purely rational perspective, it remains the only explanation reasonably available. And as Sherlock Holmes once said in relation to the pursuit of an explanation: 'Once you have removed the impossible, whatever remains, no matter how improbable, must be the truth.'

That, in essence, is what is sometimes called the cosmological argument for God's existence. That of the three possible explanations for the universe's existence, if we take into account what science and reason tell us about the universe, the third option, God, is by far the best explanation, indeed the only rational explanation.

Clue 2: a fine-tuned universe

The second clue comes from a discovery made by modern physicists, commonly referred to as the 'fine tuning' of the universe. What physicists mean when they talk about a finely tuned universe is that the fundamental physical constants and laws of the universe were, right from the very start, of the exact order or magnitude that they needed to be in order for life in the universe to exist.

To give an example, scientists tell us that had the force of the big bang at the beginning of the universe been any larger, by just the tiniest amount – a fraction of $1/10^{60}$ – then the universe would have expanded so quickly that it would have become too diverse to enable life ever to occur. Likewise, they say that if the force of the big bang had been any smaller, by the same tiny amount, the universe would have collapsed in on itself and, again, there would have been no life at all.

The degree of precision we are talking about here is astounding. A fraction of $1/10^{60}$ is improbably small – a probability so tiny, in fact, that some mathematicians would use the phrase 'mathematically impossible'. Not *logically* impossible, but for all intents and purposes, *practically* impossible.

Yet, even more incredibly, the force of the big bang is just one of more than forty different scientific constants that physicists have discovered so far, each of which had to be exactly a certain magnitude in size or power right at the very beginning of the universe in order for the universe to be capable of sustaining life. For example, had dark energy (which causes the universe to expand at an increasingly faster rate) been any greater or lesser by a fraction of $1/10^{120}$, there would be no life. To give you a sense of the magnitude of that number, it helps to bear in mind that the number of atoms in the universe is only about 10^{80}. Leonard Susskind, Professor of theoretical physics at Stanford University, says:

> The great mystery is not why there is dark energy . . . The fact that we are just on the knife edge of existence, [that] if dark energy were very much bigger, we wouldn't be here, that's the mystery.

The list of improbabilities goes on. For example, had the force of gravity been any greater or lesser by a fraction of $1/10^{40}$, there would be no life. Or had the ratio of electrons to protons in the universe been any greater or lesser by a fraction of $1/10^{37}$, there would be no life. Had only one of these many scientific constants been greater or lesser in magnitude at the universe's beginning by the tiniest margin, our universe would not have been capable of sustaining life. We would not exist. No life would. Not even simple life.

Scientists also tell us that there is no logical or scientific reason why these scientific constants all happened to be of the exact magnitude required for the universe to be life-permitting right at the beginning of the universe itself. It just so happens that, in each and every case, they were.

Think about that for a moment. If there is no God, and the universe is completely unguided, it means that each one of these constants had to have been precisely the right magnitude required, right from the very beginning of the universe, with only the unimaginably tiniest margin for error available, and all of this must have happened *completely by chance.* But for every single one of them to be exactly the right magnitude required for life to exist in the universe, *by chance,* right from the start of the universe, given the incredibly minute precision we are talking about here, defies reasonable belief. The odds have been compared to the odds of firing a bullet at a one-inch target on the other side of the observable universe, twenty billion light years away, blindfolded, and hitting the target bang on. In other words, to all intents and purposes, impossible.

Therefore, the fine-tuning of the universe is strong evidence that this life-permitting physical environment that we gratefully inhabit is not here by chance. The physicist Paul Davies, who is not a believer, writes: 'Scientists are slowly waking up to the inconvenient truth – the universe looks suspiciously like a fix.' Similarly, the atheist cosmologist Sir Fred Hoyle observes that 'a common-sense interpretation of the facts would suggest that a *super-intellect* has monkeyed with the physics and the chemistry'.

A 'multiverse' theory?

Because the fine-tuning of the universe points so compellingly towards the existence of an intelligence behind it all, as opposed to it all happening by chance, some scientists have postulated that perhaps our universe is not the only universe there is, but one of many trillions and trillions of different universes in existence. This is known as the 'multiverse theory', the most popular objection to the fine-tuning argument for God's existence. The idea here is that if there really are innumerable universes, it is not unlikely at all that at least some of them would, by chance, be as finely tuned for life as ours happens to be.

Interestingly, atheists who say they find the Christian view of the origin of the universe difficult to believe in (with its talk of God and a heaven that we cannot see) often have no difficulty believing in the multiverse theory (with its talk of other worlds and other universes that we cannot see, either).

However, as fascinating as this new theory of multiple other universes may be, their existence must, at best, remain a hypothesis, in the sense that they are, by definition, unobservable to beings within our universe, and therefore beyond the realm of direct scientific observation. There may be other universes, or there may not. But even if there are other universes, we have no basis on which to assume that the majority of them have no life, as many proponents of a multiverse theory tend to assume. It may be that all of them have life, just as ours does (the only universe that we can observe), in which case this would be even stronger evidence for a creator God. But as we don't know either way, the multiverse theory neither strengthens nor lessens the case for God.

Interestingly, prior to the discovery of the fine-tuning of the universe, there was no great scientific interest in a multiverse. Paul Davies suggests it has been the discovery that the universe is finely tuned for life – what he calls the 'Goldilocks Enigma' that has promoted a rethink. In this respect, the multiverse objection is actually a back-handed compliment to the strength of the fine-tuning argument, in that scientists recognized the fine-tuning evidence demanded an explanation and set about looking for one. But, as we have seen, there are problems in claiming that multiple other universes can be that explanation.

Clue 3: the language of God

As I mentioned earlier, Darwin did not solve, or even attempt to solve, the mystery of the origin of the first life. His theory represents an attempt to explain how we got to complex forms of life from simpler forms of life. But what about the first life? What about the first single biological cell? How do we account for that?

Advances made by the scientific community in molecular biology in recent decades, have shown us that the so-called primitive single biological cell is anything but simple. It's actually a hugely complex thing. The best way to visualize a single biological cell is to imagine that it is like a complex factory containing a boundary fence; gates; docking bays and security systems; entry facilities for raw materials; shipping facilities for finished products; internal transport systems; power plants; waste disposal plants; an army of workers with many different skills; messengers and an elaborate network of interlocking assembly lines, each of which is composed of a set of large machines that make proteins, the workhorse molecules of life. These protein machines, in turn, contain highly coordinated moving parts.

I hope that you will never look down your nose at a single biological cell ever again!

It is this incredible level of complexity that persuaded the renowned evolutionary biologist John Haldane to conclude that the first living cell could never have come into existence by chance. Haldane writes:

> Our descendants may be able to make a [single biological cell], but we must give up the idea that such an organism could have

been produced in the past, except by a similar pre-existing organism or by an agent, natural or supernatural, at least as intelligent as ourselves, and with a good deal more knowledge.

In addition to resembling the complexity of a factory, the single biological cell can do something that no man-made factory can achieve, namely reproduce itself. How does the cell know how to do this? The answer is: it comes with a blueprint! Inside each living cell, there are encoded instructions or information, telling the cell what to build and how to build it. In other words, what our advances in microbiology have discovered is that a single biological cell is not just matter, it is matter replete with information.

The significance of that last statement should not be overlooked. As Edgar Andrews, Emeritus Professor of Materials at the University of London, points out:

> We are often told that life is nothing more than organic chemistry, and that we must discard the idea that it is in some way mysterious or 'special'. But this dismissive statement ignores the inconvenient fact that life depends crucially on the storage and transmission of detailed information. Easy to overlook, perhaps, but nonetheless stupid to do so.

That information is found in the cell's nucleus, stored in the polymer molecule, deoxyribonucleic acid, better known by its abbreviated name, DNA. Along the spine of the DNA molecule, there are things that look like pegs sticking out. They constitute the bases found in a DNA molecule. It is important to know that there are only four types of those bases whose chemical names – adenine, cytosine, guanine and thymine – are commonly abbreviated in the acronym, ACGT. These four chemical pegs, when put into sequences that are recognized within the cell, become language or code or instructions.

In effect then, ACGT can be seen as the four-symbol alphabet of the language of life. It's not that it looks like a language, it is a language. This language is present in all living systems, and without it no life would be possible.

Scientists tell us that the DNA of the humble bacterium is about four million letters long. The human genome is over 3.5 billion letters long. That's 3.5 billion letters of detailed and complex instructions for how to build human beings – 3.5 billion letters of language. That's enough complex information to fill an entire library.

And the big question is where did language of that sort of complexity come from? What is the source of this language? Of course, the information that we each presently have in our DNA was passed on to us from other DNA. But the question is, what about the first living cells? Where did the information contained in *their* DNA originate from?

The only source that we know of for language is intelligence, which is why, when hieroglyphics were discovered on the Rosetta Stone and recognized as language, no one assumed natural causes. Everyone naturally and rationally inferred intelligence behind the language. Imagine if we were to discover, one day, language written on stone on the planets Mars or Jupiter. What would we infer then? Natural causes? No. We would infer that we are not the first forms of intelligent life on that planet.

The argument for God is really quite simple. It could perhaps be put like this: imagine you were on a walk in the countryside and suddenly came across an encyclopaedia lying on the ground. Would you conclude that it probably happened to be there because a nearby paper factory had exploded and all the ink, glue and paper had randomly conglomerated in the air by chance and formed this encyclopaedia lying before you? Of course not! But why not? Well, not only because of the physical unlikelihood of the components conglomerating in the air by chance to form a book, but also because when you open the book, you, as an intelligent being, quickly recognize the presence of something called 'information'. The encyclopaedia contains complex information, and wherever we come across complex information, we as intelligent beings recognize at once the work of another intelligent agent. In short, the information points us to an intelligence behind that information.

Now, as Oxford Professor John Lennox asks, given that DNA in the human genome contains more intelligent information than rooms full of encyclopaedias, is it not rational to infer intelligence behind that information as well?

In fact, this argument from information – from language in the nuclei of our biological cells – was one of the arguments that helped convert Antony Flew, who at one time was a famous academic atheist, from atheism to theism. Flew writes: 'It now seems to me that the findings of more than 50 years of scientific DNA research have provided materials for a new and enormously powerful argument to design.'

At the public announcement of the completion of the Human Genome Project, its director Frances Collins said: 'It is humbling for me and awe-inspiring to realise that we have caught the first glimpse of our own instruction book, previously known only to God.' A type of language that Collins would later go on to call 'the language of God'.

Science and faith

The irony of our age, however, is that while there are world-class scientists, like Collins, who are Christians and whose beliefs in a designer God are strengthened and supported by modern science, many laypeople still seem to think that science has somehow proved a universe without design and that we just have to accept, for that reason, that we have no one to thank for this life, as long as we have it, except chance.

But what we have seen, in this chapter, is that science has not done away with God. In fact, quite the opposite. We have seen that science and belief in God have been friends right from the very beginning and still are today. We have acknowledged that science is great but that it can't answer all the important questions of life. And we have observed that, although science can't prove or disprove God's existence, it does provide us with powerful clues pointing towards the existence of a creator God behind it all. Clues such as: the overwhelming impression of order and design; the discovery that our universe had a definite beginning; the discovery that our universe was finely tuned for life, right from the very beginning; and the discovery of semiotic information or language contained in our very own DNA.

No wonder science has inspired the faith of many in a creator God, just as belief in a creator God initially inspired the birth of modern science and continues to inspire great science even today. As James Tour, one of the world's leading nano-engineers states: 'Only a rookie who knows nothing about science would say science takes away from faith. If you really study science, it will bring you closer to God.'

9

The evidence within us
Why do I believe some things are wrong?

Simple observation of human history, sociology and literature tells us that across religions, cultures, geographies and historical epochs, human beings share this fundamental similarity: a deep and abiding moral instinct. I alluded to this instinct in Chapter 3, and to the fact that, as the philosopher Plantinga once put it: 'It is extremely difficult to be a human being and not think that some actions are right and others wrong.'

Despite that instinct, I often speak to audiences in universities, where in my experience, a large portion of the audience subscribe to the philosophical position that there is no such thing as absolute or objective moral truth. Some, for example, hold the view that morality is nothing more than a cultural construct; and others, that it is an illusion brought about by our genes – an evolutionary adaptation – whose purpose is simply to aid our survival. However, despite a reticence to acknowledge the existence of objective moral truths that have real claims over our life, rarely do I find, even in such audiences, people who are unwilling to agree with me when I say that torturing innocent people for fun is absolutely wrong, that genocide is absolutely wrong or that child abuse is absolutely wrong, and that these things would still be wrong even if laws were passed that legalized such actions and all their friends came to believe these things to be right and good. Why is that?

Shortly after the Second World War, leading Nazi officers, responsible for atrocities committed in the dreaded concentration camps, were tried in Nuremberg by the International Criminal

Court. They were condemned as guilty of punishment even though, as the officers' defence lawyers argued, these men were simply acting in accordance with the law of their land at the time. Why? Because the judges of the International Criminal Court recognized a higher law to which we are all accountable. One that cannot be erased simply with the stroke of a legislative pen or a shift in public opinion.

As human beings, we intuitively recognize the existence of this higher law: a moral law to which we are all accountable. Christians believe this moral intuition that we possess is something that God has implanted in us, and that it is an important part of what makes us human – the ability not only to be aware of the objective categories of 'is' and 'isn't', but also of 'good' and 'evil', 'right' and 'wrong', 'ought' and 'ought not'.

Some people object to the claim that there is an objective moral law that applies to everyone on the basis that, if there really were one, people wouldn't disagree with each other on moral issues, as we often do. However, while it is true that people have moral disagreements with each other all the time, have you noticed how, when we do have such disagreements, we still make appeals to some objective standard of morality? For example, when Mr Jones says, 'It was wrong of Mr Smith to do X,' and Mr Smith says, 'It wasn't wrong of me to do X,' the only reason that Mr Jones and Mr Smith can even have a moral disagreement with each other is because both of them believe in such a thing as right and wrong to be right or wrong about.

It's just like people who argue about whether a footballer has committed a foul. Their disagreement about whether a foul has been committed doesn't call into question the existence of such a thing as the rules of football. On the contrary, it affirms it. For it makes no sense to disagree about whether a foul has been committed if there is no such thing as the rules of football to fall foul of. Similarly, moral disagreements don't call into question the existence of an objective moral law. They affirm it. For there's no point in a moral disagreement if there's no objective morality to disagree about in the first place.

Morality as evidence for God

I mentioned in an earlier chapter how atheists sometimes point to the existence of evil in the world, such as terrorism or Hitler's concentration camps, as proof that an all-powerful and all-good God cannot exist. And I explained why this argument, known as the logical problem of evil, is no longer considered by philosophers to be a persuasive argument.

Indeed, one might argue: not only does the existence of evil not disprove God's existence, it points to it in the sense that, if we assert that something is morally evil or wrong, we must also assume there is an objective moral law by which to recognize that rightness or wrongness. But if we assume an objective moral law, must we not also posit an 'objective-moral-law giver'? And who but God could be that objective-moral-law giver?

The argument, which is called the moral argument for God's existence, can be put more formally as such:

- **premise 1:** if God did not exist, objective moral duties would not exist;
- **premise 2:** objective moral duties do exist;
- **conclusion:** God exists.

As you can see, it is a strong argument because in order to defeat it, you either have to defeat premise 1 or premise 2 – that is, you either have to explain how objective moral duties could exist without God, or you have to deny that objective moral duties exist at all, both of which are very difficult to do. Therefore, atheists would have to take the view either that there are no objective moral duties or objective moral duties do exist but they are grounded in something other than God.

No objective morality?

Probably the most famous atheist to have held the view that there is no objective morality is Nietzsche. Nietzsche reasoned that, having removed God from the picture, we must recognize that we have also removed the only objective reference point for deciding what is right and what is wrong. The existentialist atheist Sartre made the same point when he said: 'If God does not exist, there disappears with Him all possibility of finding values in an intelligible heaven.'

If these atheist philosophers are correct, and there are no objective moral duties, it raises the question: why, then, does almost everyone act as if there are?

One explanation, given by atheist thinkers such as John Gray, is, while it is true we have what appears to be a very deeply ingrained sense that there is an objective moral law, in reality it is an illusion brought about by our genes; it is an illusion that will enhance our chances of survival.

The philosopher of science Michael Ruse describes the position like this:

The position of the modern evolutionist . . . is that humans have an awareness of morality . . . because such an awareness is of biological worth. Morality is a biological adaptation no less than are hands and feet and teeth . . . Considered as a rationally justifiable set of claims about an objective something, ethics is illusory. I appreciate that when somebody says, 'Love thy neighbour as thyself,' they think they are referring above and beyond themselves . . . Nevertheless . . . such reference is truly without foundation. Morality is just an aid to survival and reproduction . . . and any deeper meaning is illusory . . .

Dawkins made a similar point in an interview with a British journalist when he stated that our deeply held belief that rape is wrong is just as arbitrary as the fact that we developed five fingers rather than six. However, this perspective on morality – as nothing more than an evolutionary aid to survival and reproduction – goes against our deepest human instincts. Why? Because most of us think that when it comes to beliefs such as our belief that rape is wrong, we really do apprehend objective moral duties. As Ruse himself confesses: 'The man who says that it is morally acceptable to rape little children is just as mistaken as the man who says $2 + 2 = 5$.'

Besides, running contrary to our deepest moral intuitions, another challenge to the view that morality is nothing but an evolutionary aid to survival, is that it also undermines rationality itself. Here is the argument: if we believe that there is no God (and that our mind and its perception of reality are controlled entirely by our genes which are themselves geared towards the evolutionary aims of survival), we can no longer trust our deepest moral instincts and reasoning because we would have to assume that our minds, controlled by our genes, are geared, primarily, towards survival rather than truth – and whatever it might be that aids our survival. And, interestingly, Gray concedes exactly this point when he writes that 'the human mind serves evolutionary success, not truth'.

However, if that is the case, what about Gray's own mind? We must conclude, if we believe him, that his act of writing this sentence ('the human mind serves evolutionary success, not truth') itself serves evolutionary success, not truth. But if that's true, why should we believe anything he says?

Do you see the problem? To assert as true the proposition that the human mind doesn't serve truth is nonsense. It's self-defeating. It's the philosophical equivalent of sawing off the very branch that you are sitting on. This is the problem with the theory that our thoughts and intuitions about reality are, in essence, nothing but the unwitting servants of evolutionary success – it undermines not only the rationality of the theory, but rationality itself.

An objective morality without God?

Other atheist philosophers, unwilling to accept the claim that bad things such as racism, sexism and child abuse are not objectively wrong, have tried to affirm objective moral values in the absence of God by grounding them elsewhere.

Reason as a foundation for morality?

For example, the prominent modern moral philosopher John Finnis argues that it is a foundational principle that no one should intentionally harm the well-being of another. Why? Because, he argues, it would be unreasonable for us, if we value our own well-being, to harm the well-being of others intentionally because intelligence and reasonableness help us recognize that our own well-being cannot have a higher value than that of others, simply because it is our own.

The weakness of such a theory, however, is that it gives no account of why fundamental impartiality should be a moral obligation. Finnis simply assumes that intelligence and reasonableness will recognize that one's own well-being is of no more value than another's. But why? For example, Mr Jones might believe that all human beings are equally valuable, whereas Mr Smith might believe that his own well-being is actually of more value to him than, say, Mr Jones's well-being. Or Mr Smith might think that his child is more valuable to him than Mr Jones's well-being. And if that's the case, it is not necessarily unreasonable nor illogical for him to harm Mr Jones intentionally in order to achieve something of great importance to himself or to someone he loves.

Reason is wonderful, but as a foundation for morality, it is not sufficient. There is no logical formula that proves we should not be self-interested in our actions, nor is there a syllogism which demonstrates we should value the well-being of others as much as our own. As Kai Nielsen, one of the most prominent atheists in Canada, observes: pure practical reason, even with a good knowledge of the facts, will not take you to morality. He writes:

> We have not been able to show that reason requires the moral point of view, or that all really rational persons, unhoodwinked by myth or ideology, need not be individual egoists or classical amoralists. Reason doesn't decide here. The picture I have painted for you is not a pleasant one. Reflection on it depresses me . . . Pure practical reason, even with a good knowledge of the facts, will not take you to morality.

Our humanity towards others as a foundation for morality?

Another prominent moral philosopher who attempts to build a non-religious foundation for morality is Ronald Dworkin. Dworkin argues that we almost all accept that human life is sacred. For some of us, he says, it is on the basis of religious faith; and for others, it is on the basis of the deep secular belief that 'although the cosmic process is bereft of meaning, every human life is nonetheless a masterpiece of natural and human creation'.

Dworkin's foundation for objective morality then is the great value that *we* attach to every human being understood as a creative masterpiece. But to whom is Dworkin referring when he says 'we'? Of course, most modern Western liberals would nod their heads and agree that, 'yes, "we" attach great value to every human being'. But what about the Nazis? Did the Nazis value the Jews intrinsically? Or the Turks the Armenians? Or the Hutus the Tutsis?

The problem with Dworkin's foundation for morality is that it assumes a consensus among human agents that the anthropological evidence suggests does not exist.

As the renowned anthropologist Claude Lévi-Strauss states:

> The concept of an all-inclusive humanity, which makes no distinction between races or cultures, appeared very late in the history of mankind and did not spread very widely across the face of the globe . . . For the majority of the human species, and for tens of thousands of years, the idea that humanity includes every human being on the face of the earth does not exist at all. The designation stops at the border of each tribe.

Even Aristotle, the great moral philosopher of Classical Greece, did not support the idea of the equal dignity of all human beings. Like his contemporaries, he saw women and slaves as naturally inferior beings.

As historians and political philosophers such as Tom Holland, Larry Siedentop and Jürgen Habermas have all pointed out in their writings, the notion of human dignity and the equality of all human beings is not a universally accepted notion. Historically speaking, it is a product of Judaism and Christianity, both of which state that human beings are creatures made in the image of God. As Holland explains:

> People in the West, even those who may imagine that they have emancipated themselves from Christian belief, in fact, are shot through with Christian assumptions about almost everything . . . All of us in the West are a goldfish, and the water that we swim in is Christianity, by which I don't necessarily mean the confessional form of the faith, but, rather, considered as an entire civilisation.

As much as we may wish it to be true that we can build a morality on the fact that everyone considers human life to be sacred (as Dworkin claims), the unfortunate truth is that it is not the case that every person and culture on the planet accepts this idea. There simply is no universal 'we' affirming the sanctity of every human life.

Science as a foundation for morality?

It has recently been asserted by popular atheist writers that science now provides us with an adequate foundation for morality even though, as far as I'm aware, there aren't any serious philosophers who would argue that position.

A good part of the reason why few, if any, philosophers consider science an adequate foundation for morality is because, as David Hume pointed out long ago, no matter how hard you try, no amount of reasoning can get you from a description of the way things are in the world (which is the province of science) to a prescription of the way things ought to be in the world (which is the province of morality). Those who attempt to do so are committing what is known in philosophy as the 'is/ought fallacy': the mistake of trying to make the impossible logical leap from 'what is' to 'what ought to be'.

Oxford professor Lennox rather humorously puts the point across like this:

> Science can tell us that if you put strychnine in your grandmother's tea it will kill her. But Science cannot tell you whether you ought or ought not to do so in order to get your hands on her property.

Nevertheless, in a book written by the New Atheist writer Sam Harris entitled *The Moral Landscape: How science can determine human values*, Dawkins provides the following endorsement:

> I was one of those who had unthinkingly bought into the hectoring myth that science can say nothing about morals.

Sam Harris's book *The Moral Landscape* has changed all that for me. Moral philosophers, too, will find their world exhilaratingly turned upside down, as they discover a need to learn some neuroscience. As for religion, and the preposterous idea that we need God to be good, nobody wields a sharper bayonet than Sam Harris.

So, what novel argument does Harris employ that has changed Dawkins's mind? Harris maintains:

We simply must stand somewhere. I am arguing that, in the moral sphere, it is safe to begin with the premise that it is good to avoid behaving in such a way as to produce the worst possible misery for every one – hence promoting well-being.

And with that premise as a given, he goes on to suggest ways in which neuroscience might, in the future, provide us with ways of measuring that well-being.

You may be wondering how Harris has avoided the problem of the 'is/ought fallacy'? The answer is: he hasn't. He simply assumes that objective moral duties exist, and that the foundational moral duty is to minimize misery to everyone. The trouble is, whatever got him to that starting assumption, it's not science. So, it just isn't true to say that science underpins the foundations of Harris's theory. In reality, his foundational moral truth is nothing more than an assertion. And it is only after making the assertion that we *ought to* minimize harm to everyone that he then goes on to bring in some science.

As the evolutionary biologist and outspoken atheist P. Z. Myers objects:

I don't think Harris's criterion – that we can use science to justify maximising the well-being of individuals – is valid.

We can't. We can certainly use science to say how we can maximise well-being, once we define well-being . . . although even that might be a bit more slippery than he portrays it . . . Harris is smuggling in an unscientific prior in his category of well-being.

Harris brings in the science to work out how best to achieve his foundational moral truth, but the most essential question is: on what basis is his foundational moral truth justified? Because, what if someone questions his 'unscientific prior' – the assumption that it is good to avoid behaving in such a way as to produce the worst possible misery for everyone? What if somebody like Hitler decides that we should modify Harris's ethical starting point by excluding people of certain races or ethnicities from the list of those whom we should avoid harming and making miserable? Hitler too had certain fundamental unscientific assertions, and, like Harris, he also called on science as a tool to advance his fundamental assertions. If science really is the foundation here, on what scientific basis can we say that Hitler's starting point is wrong and Harris's starting point is right?

We find ourselves stumbling over the inevitable philosophical weakness of any ethical system grounded in a so-called self-evident moral principle: that any stated principle used to underpin that ethical system might be said to be nothing more than an arbitrary or subjective assertion being made by the individual founder of that system. This is the original problem raised by Nietzsche against those who would try to hold on to the idea of an objective morality without reference to God: if God is dead, who speaks? Well, it has to be humankind, because without God, 'Man is the measure of all things,' as Protagoras famously said. But then the next question becomes – which man or woman? Which human being? Sam Harris or Adolf Hitler? Mother Teresa or Josef Stalin? You or me?

Objective morality as a brute fact?

Some atheist thinkers have tried to argue that it is just a brute fact about the universe that some kinds of actions are morally right and others morally wrong: that is to say, we cannot explain why kindness is right and cruelty is wrong, they just are.

The major difficulty with this view, however, as the atheist philosopher J. L. Mackie points out, is that it would be very strange or 'queer' for moral facts somehow just to 'exist' in an impersonal and purposeless universe in which everything ultimately reduces to the basic particles of physics.

We may comprehend how scientific laws can exist in a universe that boils down to the basic particles of physics, for scientific laws simply describe what happens in our universe. They represent observations about things that happen with consistent regularity. Yet, scientific laws *describe*, whereas moral laws *prescribe*. They tell us not how things are, but how things ought to be: how we ought to live. But why should we think an impersonal universe would generate an opinion about anything, let alone an opinion about how we live our lives?

The very nature of morality is a judgment about how we ought to act, think and speak. But let me ask you this: how can we have judgments without a judge? How can we have an opinion without a mind? How can we have morality in this universe without a personality behind it? For that which is impersonal, without a mind, neither knows nor cares.

As Chesterton writes:

If there has been from the beginning anything that could possibly be called a purpose, it must reside in something that has the elements of a person. There cannot be a purpose or an intention hovering in the air all by itself, any more than a memory that nobody remembers.

It seems to me that if atheism is right, and this universe is ultimately impersonal and purposeless; one giant machine of unguided cause and effect that came *from* nothing, *by* nothing and is *for* nothing – then what it has to say about how we live our lives is, and can be, nothing.

Furthermore, even if the impossible were possible, and an impersonal universe could somehow generate moral truths, what would that even look like in meaningful experience? Take, for example, the moral obligation not to torture innocent people for fun. Let us assume an impersonal universe has somehow generated an objective moral law that says torturing innocent people for fun is wrong. Well, let us now imagine a situation where an emperor or monarch with absolute and total power over his or her citizens has a penchant for doing exactly that – torturing innocent citizens for fun. What would it mean for that emperor that this moral obligation exists? And what difference would it make if he just ignored this moral obligation generated by an impersonal universe? It is hard enough to know what it is for an objective moral law just to exist as a mere abstraction, sort of just floating out there somewhere in the universe, dictating how we should live our lives; harder still to grasp what practical authority it has over those who should feel themselves disinclined to follow it.

To look to an impersonal universe for a moral reality makes no sense. We do not condemn hurricanes for destroying houses, nor meteors for colliding into planets, nor even cats for torturing mice. Morality is a property only and ever associated with persons.

Trying to account for an objective moral law without an objective-moral-law giver is a bit like trying to imagine a story without a storyteller or a judgment without a judge: it just doesn't make sense. In contrast, the existence of a personal and moral God behind the existence of this universe makes eminent sense in combination with an objective moral law.

Euthyphro objection

An objection that atheists sometimes raise against the idea of God as the source of an objective moral law is that it seems to make morality arbitrary. We feel the weight of this criticism in a question that Socrates famously posed to Euthyphro – often referred to as the 'Euthyphro dilemma' which, roughly paraphrased, was: is something good because God wills it, or does God will it because it is good? The problem with the first option is that it seems to make morality arbitrary, implying that morality is just whatever God commands, no matter what he commands. The problem with the second option is that it seems to constrain God, by making his will subject to an authority even greater than him; a problem especially acute for Christians, who understand that there is no authority greater than God.

Christian philosopher William Alston argues that what Euthyphro should have said to Socrates is: 'There is a third option, namely that God wills what he does not because it is good, but because *he* is good.' In other words, goodness itself comes from God. So, goodness and God's will can never be in conflict.

Christianity holds that goodness is not merely an illusion, nor a human invention, nor an abstraction floating free in an impersonal universe: it is real – rooted and grounded in a person. The person of God. In contrast to the moral vacuity of atheism, the existence of a morally good God offers a far better and more satisfying explanation for objective morality – and of our own awareness of this objective reality, as beings created in the image of this morally good God.

Don't stop believing

If, like most people, you believe in an objective moral law – that some things really are right and other things wrong, then perhaps this chapter has helped you to see that your belief makes absolute sense in a universe in which you and I are not here by accident, but here on purpose because God wanted us to be here and has an opinion about how we should live our lives in this universe he created. If you are a committed atheist, this chapter may have caused you to doubt your belief, either in the existence of an objective moral law or in the non-existence of God. I certainly hope it's the latter. The last thing our world needs is more people who, like Nietzsche, don't believe that genocide, child abuse or racism is objectively wrong. For whatever a philosopher may think about a person who cannot recognize such things as truly evil, a psychologist would have very grave concerns indeed.

Besides, which of us could doubt the existence of morality even if we tried? Which of us could doubt that cruelty is wrong and that acts of kindness are good? We can no more doubt the existence of a moral law than we can doubt the existence of scientific laws. Both are true, both are important. Our understanding of life is incomplete without either. And, revealingly, the existence of God makes sense of both. He makes sense of life in all its entirety.

10

The evidence of history
Is the Jesus story fact or fiction?

Which God?

So far, we have looked at reasons and evidence for the existence of God. But why would we conclude, if there is a creator God, that it is the Christian God?

For Christians, the primary answer to that question is, 'because of Jesus Christ'. If God exists, and the evidence we have looked at strongly suggests that he does, the next question becomes: 'Has he spoken?' Christianity answers that question with a resounding: 'Yes! He has spoken to us, and most clearly so in Jesus.'

Christianity claims that Jesus was and is God, come in human flesh. Just think about that for a moment. That God would choose to enter our space-time human history as one of us. That, in Jesus, God ate and drank; sweated and got tired; suffered pain and felt human emotions – love, joy, sadness. That he had normal human experiences of growing up in a family, of having a job, of being tempted; and painful human experiences of bereavement, betrayal, torture and, finally, crucifixion.

This is the great miracle which Christians call the 'Incarnation': that God most high, compelled by love, would stoop so low, and enter our world to be born as one of us, to live among us, and to suffer and die for us, in order to rescue us from ourselves, only to rise again, in order to rescue us from death. Lewis uses the remarkable analogy of a diver to illustrate the wonder of this divine descent and resurrection:

One has the picture of a diver, stripping off garment after garment, making himself naked, then flashing for a moment in the air, and then down through the green, and warm, and sunlit water into the pitch black, cold, freezing water, down into the mud and slime, then up again, his lungs almost bursting, back again to the green and warm and sunlit water, and then at last out into the sunshine, holding in his hand the dripping thing he went down to get. This thing is human nature.

The idea here is that Jesus came into the world to rescue and revive us not only morally, intellectually and emotionally; but also spiritually. As Chesterton observes: 'Jesus didn't come into the world to make bad people good, he came to make dead people live.'

The uniqueness of Jesus Christ

I sometimes meet people who are surprised to discover that Jesus was a real person. A lot of people assume he is some sort of mythical figure or legend. But as far as historians are concerned, the fact that Jesus really existed is non-contentious. The historian John Dickson states that believing Jesus never existed is the historical equivalent of denying the moon landing. And biblical scholar Bart Ehrman, who is not a Christian, writes that virtually every scholar of antiquity, of biblical studies, of classics and of Christian origins agrees that Jesus existed.

With Christianity representing the number-one belief system in the world (in terms of its overall number of followers), Jesus' vast and lasting impact on humanity and human history is incontrovertible. In addition to having the largest following of any leader, there has been no one else who has achieved the level of cross-cultural, trans-ethnic impact that Jesus has had – including among those who are not Christians.

Albert Einstein once said the following in an interview:

No man can deny the fact that Jesus existed. I am a Jew, but I am enthralled by the luminous figure of the Nazarene. No one can read the Gospels without feeling the actual presence of Jesus. His personality pulsates in every word. No myth is filled with such life.

The life and teachings of Jesus have not only had a profound impact on the West, but also on Africa, South America and Asia – the parts of the world where most Christians now live. Jesus himself came from the part of the world that touches Africa, Asia and Europe.

His teachings are widely acknowledged to be the greatest that have ever fallen from the lips of a human being: love your neighbour as yourself. Do to others what you would have them do to you. Love your enemy. Turn the other cheek.

Even many atheists regard his words as the greatest words ever spoken. John Mortimer, the well-known barrister and writer who created the series *Rumpole of the Bailey* – and an outspoken atheist – says that 'it's beyond doubt that society must return to Jesus' teaching as a system of ethics if we are to avoid social disasters'.

As a lawyer, I can say that our Western legal system, which is admired across the world, did not just come out of a philosophical or ethical vacuum. Although it is rarely acknowledged nowadays, our legal system is founded on Judeo-Christian ethics. Many of our laws were originally based on the teachings of Jesus. The law of negligence, for example – which establishes that we each owe a duty of care to avoid acts that could reasonably be foreseen as likely to injure others – is based directly on Jesus' teaching that we are to love our neighbour.

Speaking of Jesus' moral influence on our planet, the famous historian and self-professed sceptic W. E. H. Lecky writes:

The character of Jesus has not only been the highest pattern of virtue, but the longest incentive in its practice, and has exerted so deep an influence, that it may be truly said that the simple record of three short years of active life has done more to regenerate and to soften mankind than all the disquisitions of philosophers and all the exhortations of moralists.

Even the history-changing Napoleon Bonaparte is said to have remarked that:

Between [Jesus] and every other person in the world there is no possible term of comparison. Alexander, Caesar, Charlemagne, and myself founded empires; but upon what foundation did we rest the creations of our genius? Upon force. Jesus Christ founded an empire upon love; and at this hour millions of men would die for Him.

This incredible and unequalled level of historical impact surely requires an explanation. Especially when we bear in mind that Jesus wasn't wealthy, wasn't a politician, had no army, never travelled far from home and was killed when he was only thirty-three years old, in the most humiliating fashion possible: hung naked on a cross to die in full public spectacle. In a shame and honour culture such as it was back then, this inglorious ending should have spelled the complete disintegration of any movement he was trying to bring about. Yet, 2,000 years later, over two billion people self-identify as his followers. We even speak of historical events in terms of what happened 'before him' (BC) and 'after him' (AD).

Something truly extraordinary must have happened after his death to explain all this. To which the Christian response is: 'Something truly extraordinary did happen: Jesus rose from the dead.'

Some people may respond to this Christian claim by saying: 'OK sure, I concede that Jesus obviously existed and made a big impact. Historians don't doubt it, fine. But why do you have to get all weird and supernatural about it all, claiming that Jesus was God? Why can't we just say he was a very good moral teacher who did and said some good moral things and leave it at that?'

Well, the appropriate answer here is that we can't do that because Jesus himself won't let us. Consider the claims that he made about himself. While other religious leaders taught people a way to live, Jesus said, 'I am the way'. While other religious leaders taught people a truth to believe, Jesus said, 'I am the truth'. And while other religious leaders taught people how to live a fulfilled life, Jesus said, 'I am the life'.

In Jesus, you encounter a man who not only claimed that his word was the most important in the whole world, you get a man who claimed that by his word, he made the whole world. Distinct from all other major religious leaders, Jesus not only taught about God, he claimed, by his words and by his actions, to be God.

We can't simply dismiss such claims as the claims of a good moral teacher. For, if it were anyone else, these claims would sound like the ravings of a mad man or a megalomaniac.

As many preachers have pointed out, given what he said, Jesus was either a liar, a lunatic or the Lord (or a mad man, bad man or God-man, as others have put it). In any case, what we cannot do is simply call him a good moral teacher and leave it at that.

Lewis writes:

A man who was merely a man and said the sort of things Jesus said wouldn't be a great moral teacher; he'd either be insane or else he'd be the devil of hell. You must make your choice. Either this man was and is the Son of God or else insane or something worse. But don't let us come up with any patronising nonsense about his being a great human teacher. He hasn't left that open to us. He didn't intend to.

Could he have been a lunatic? Whatever you might say about Jesus' teaching, what you cannot say is that this is the teaching of a madman; for his teaching is almost universally recognized as brilliant and profound. From their perspective as psychiatrists, Pablo Martínez and Andrew Sims (former President of the Royal College of Psychiatrists) apply a series of tests to examine Christ's mental health based on his words, actions, relationship with others, reactions when facing adversity, and influence on people. They conclude: 'Jesus was not only a man with a balanced personality, but he also lived a totally righteous life . . . The words and deeds of Jesus plainly indicate extraordinary mental health and unequivocal moral uprightness.' They also observe: 'If Jesus had been psychotic, most likely he would not have died nailed to the cross as a malefactor, but instead would have been abandoned in the streets.'

Clearly, Jesus was not insane. But if not a mad man, could he have been a bad man? A sort of religious conman?

We read that Jesus travelled, ate, spoke and lived with his disciples virtually 24/7 for three years and never once did they see him do anything wrong. If they had, they would never have believed he was God. No conman, no matter how good, could keep up a pretence for that long given that degree of continual proximity and openness.

And although his own life was faultless, Jesus was known as the friend of sinners because he associated with those who were shunned by society – prostitutes, lepers, tax collectors – Jesus had time for them all. And given their life experiences, these were probably people quite adept at recognizing phoneys and smelling lies.

Jesus even had time for the little children as well and wasn't swayed by the demand of the crowds or of the powerful. The only people he wasn't popular with were the religious rulers of his day, and yet even his worst detractors could not point an accusing finger at him. He could ask the religious leaders: 'Which one of you can convict me of any sin?' and leave them standing speechless. When he stood on trial before the Roman Governor of Judea, Pontius Pilate, even he came to the conclusion that this man had done no wrong. Pilate pleaded repeatedly with the crowd to let Jesus go free. Even when Jesus was being tortured, at the end of his physical limits, the words that uttered forth from his lips were: 'Father, forgive them, for they do not know what they are doing' (Luke 23.34, NIV). For all these reasons, the Russian author Dostoevsky described Jesus as 'infinitely beautiful'.

How could such a person ever be described as a bad man?

Perhaps the most important fact to be decided concerning the question as to whether Jesus really was God or not is this: did he rise from the dead, as he said he would? This is a crucial question. Did he really come back from the grave? Because, if Jesus really rose from the dead, as he said he would, then it makes sense to believe everything he had to say about himself. But if he didn't rise from the dead, then it makes little sense to believe he really was God, despite the beauty of his words and actions.

In other words, we have to make a decision here. There is no middle ground. He either was God or he wasn't, and which it is depends very much on whether he stayed dead, as dead men do, or whether he truly rose from the dead on the third day, as he claimed that he would. Even the apostle Paul is happy to admit that if Jesus didn't rise from the dead, it would make no sense for us to believe in him as Lord, no matter how profound his teachings. In one of his letters recorded in the New Testament, he writes: 'If Christ has not been raised, our preaching is useless and so is your faith . . . If only for this life we have hope in Christ, we are of all people most to be pitied' (1 Corinthians 15.14, 19, NIV).

The resurrection

So, does it make any sense for an educated person, living in the twenty-first century, to believe in the historical resurrection of Jesus Christ?

Some would say, 'Of course not!' Because, let's face it, to believe he rose from the dead is to believe something extraordinary for which there is no proof because we are making claims about an event that happened almost 2,000 years ago.

However, while it is true that we are talking about an event that happened 2,000 years ago, there are many other events that happened in ancient history that we are certain occurred, such as the fall of Rome, the conquests of Alexander the Great, the death of Socrates and the battle of Thermopylae. If we were to label any belief irrational, merely on the basis that it concerns an event in ancient history, we would be labelling irrational a good proportion of beliefs that we have about our world, effectively erasing a sizeable proportion of the education curriculum.

I want to suggest that, provided one is not so sceptical as to discount historical studies entirely, and provided one is open-minded enough to investigate and consider the historical evidence for the resurrection of Jesus Christ, there is a very compelling case for the historicity of the resurrection to be made.

Believing in miracles

However, I often hear people say: 'Look! I don't care what evidence you think you have for the resurrection. I don't even need to look at it. Because "I know that I know that I know" that people just don't rise from the dead. It's against the laws of nature and therefore completely impossible.'

So, before we examine the evidence for the resurrection, let's consider this objection to belief in the resurrection – the objection that miracles are impossible. Is it really a rational objection? The argument, put a little bit more formally, looks something like this:

- **premise 1:** everything that happens is the result of uniform natural laws;
- **premise 2:** a miracle (an event that is inexplicable by uniform natural laws) would be a violation of premise 1;
- **conclusion:** miracles never happen.

But the problem with this argument is that it is circular because the statement *everything that happens is the result of uniform natural laws* (premise 1), is just another way of saying that *miracles never happen* (conclusion). In other words, the argument begins by asserting the very thing which it is trying to prove. In logic, this kind of circularity is therefore considered a formal fallacy. So when someone argues that miracles never happen because the laws of nature explain everything, they are actually not making an argument at all. At most, they are simply asserting and reasserting a particular worldview known as atheistic naturalism, which (as mentioned in Chapter 7) is a worldview that assumes that the entirety of existence can be explained as a closed, self-contained system of natural causes.

Like atheistic naturalism, Christianity also understands that we live in a system of uniform natural causes, such as gravity (Isaac Newton was a Christian after all). It's just that, like Newton, Christians believe that this system of uniform natural causes is not a closed system but an open one – a system that is open to inter-vention by God, the Creator of the system. In fact, the very word itself – 'miracle' – actually presupposes, rather than sets aside, the idea that nature operates according to consistent and ordered natural laws because if it didn't, there would be nothing striking or surprising about miracles when they do occur.

If you studied philosophy, you may have encountered a much more sophisticated argument against miracles posed by the enlightenment philosopher Hume. It is an argument against belief in miracles, based not on their impossibility but on their improbability.

Hume's best argument against the rationality of believing in miracles goes something like this: based on our general knowledge and observation of the way the world operates (that is, the fact that every day we observe countless events, all of which are explicable by uniform natural laws), the intrinsic probability of a miracle is so extraordinarily small that it could never be rational to believe in a miracle based on human testimony.

Using similar reasoning to Hume's, New Testament critic Bart Ehrman argues:

> Historians can only establish what probably happened in the past, and by definition a miracle is the least probable occurrence. And so, by the very canons of historical research, we can't claim that a miracle probably happened. By definition it probably didn't.

If Hume and Ehrman are correct, it would seem that historical studies could never support the validity of miracle claims such as the resurrection. However, they are not correct, as other philosophers have since pointed out. The error of Hume's argument is this: Hume deduces that because the prior probability of miracles, generally speaking, is extremely low, the probability that any specific miracle claim is true must also be extremely low. It sounds logical, but it's not. The reason this argument is flawed is because circumstantial evidence can render what would be an otherwise inherently improbable event very probable.

You can demonstrate this using Bayes's probability analysis, commonly known as 'Bayes's theorem', which is a mathematical formula that philosophers and scientists use to estimate probabilities. That of course would be quite technical and interest only the mathematicians who are reading this book. But actually, the idea that circumstantial evidence can render what would be an otherwise inherently improbable event very probable is something that most people recognize intuitively given some examples.

For instance, if the inherent probability of event X occurring at any given instance was the only thing we ever took into account in determining whether event X has occurred in a particular instance, then we would be led into denying the reliability of many everyday items of news we read in the newspapers. For example, we would deny that Bob Edwards really was struck by lightning for the third time in his life as reported in *The Times*, or that Jill Smith really did win the lottery for a second time in her life as reported in *The Guardian*. But as it is, we actually do believe such items of news as they are reported, even though the probability of an individual being struck by lightning three times or winning the lottery twice is extremely low. Why? Because we also take into account, whether consciously or not, the evidence surrounding these specific events, including the unlikelihood of the newspaper reporting such hugely improbable events if they did not really happen.

By the way, a man named Bob Edwards of North Carolina really has been struck by lightning three times, once in 1997, once in 2009 and once in 2012. This is a man you don't want to get overly close to as a friend.

What is interesting is that our legal system also operates on this same understanding of probability and evidence. Its judges especially are aware that circumstantial evidence can render what would be an otherwise inherently improbable event very probable. In one case in 2008, a judge of the Privy Council provided a memorable illustration to demonstrate how this works. She explained that if a man walking in Regent's Park in London claims to have seen a lion in the park, then in all probability, he was mistaken. It was probably just a big dog. However, if further evidence is brought to light, such as the fact that the lion's cage at London Zoo (which is next to Regent's Park) is open, and that there is no lion in said cage as there should be, then it is probable now that the man did, indeed, see a lion. In other words, the circumstantial evidence surrounding the claim has rendered what would ordinarily be a hugely improbable event actually rather probable.

This is why good lawyers, philosophers, mathematicians and scientists all recognize, methodologically, that claims like these must be considered on a case-by-case basis. You can't just ignore the evidence. Therefore, rationally speaking, there is no a priori argument against establishing a miracle, historically.

As the modern theologian Wolfhart Pannenberg points out:

> If somebody considers it with David Hume . . . to be a general rule, suffering no exception, that the dead remain dead, then of course one cannot accept the Christian assertion that Jesus was raised. But then this is not a historical judgment but an ideological belief.

In other words, good historians, like lawyers, should be willing to go wherever the evidence leads. Which brings us back to our question.

What is the evidence for the resurrection?

Investigating the evidence for the resurrection

In order to be as impartial as possible, let us only consider as evidence those historical facts concerning Jesus Christ which virtually every serious historian acknowledges, whether Christian, atheist, agnostic or otherwise.

Thanks to the work of scholars, this is something we are in a position to do. I refer in particular to the work of Gary R. Habermas and Michael R. Licona who, between them, have collated and analysed over 3,500 scholarly works and articles – virtually everything written by academic historians since 1975 on the events surrounding Jesus' life, death and resurrection – so as to determine the historical facts on which everyone agrees.

What their work demonstrates is that virtually every serious historian, whether Christian, atheist, agnostic or otherwise, acknowledges the following three minimal facts about Jesus Christ: first, that he died by crucifixion; second, that his disciples genuinely believed that Jesus rose from the dead and appeared to them on a number of occasions; and third, that the early Church exploded in numbers soon after Jesus' death. Actually, there are more than just those three agreed facts we could turn to as evidence in support of the resurrection, but to keep things simple, I will stick with just those three facts.

Investigating the case for the resurrection then involves assessing which of the available hypotheses makes most sense in light of these agreed baseline facts. Incidentally, this is essentially what judges do with the evidence presented to them in a court of law. Judges decide what validly constitutes the evidence, and then they make inferences from the evidence to the best explanation for the evidence. The technical word for this process of reasoning is called 'abduction'. It also happens to be the same type of reasoning Sherlock Holmes uses in solving all his cases.

Of course, if the resurrection happened, it would fit these agreed historical facts perfectly. That is, if the resurrection happened, it would explain why it is that Jesus' disciples genuinely believed that Jesus rose from the dead and appeared to them on a number of occasions; and it would make sense of why the early Church exploded in numbers soon after.

But here's the challenge: if there is a plausible naturalistic alternative for these agreed facts of history, then the resurrection claim is unlikely to be true, at least from an historical standpoint.

Alternative theories

What, then, are the alternative hypotheses? Well, if Jesus did not rise from the dead as Christians believe, then it means that his disciples, who said that he did, were *deceivers*, *deceived* or *deluded*.

Could the disciples have deceived everyone? The answer is, 'Certainly not'. Besides the fact that they would have had to steal the body to hoax a resurrection, which was virtually impossible given that the tomb was sealed with a boulder and kept under Roman guard, historians are in almost unanimous agreement that the disciples sincerely believed they saw a risen Jesus. Why? Because of the fact that the disciples refused to back down on their claim that he had risen, even after persecution, torture and execution. And, as historians recognize, nothing proves sincerity more than martyrdom. People don't willingly sacrifice everything for something they know to be a lie, especially when they know that there is nothing to be gained if it is a lie. The first disciples had nothing to gain from making up a lie about Jesus' resurrection but everything to lose, including their reputation, friendships, social standing, safety and even their own lives.

But if the disciples weren't lying, they may have been deceived. Is this a plausible explanation? Well, you have to ask: 'Who would have wanted to deceive them?' Not the Romans. They wouldn't have wanted to create a legend that would challenge Rome's authority. Nor the Jewish leaders. They wanted Jesus dead because he was challenging their religious authority.

Perhaps Jesus himself deceived everybody and didn't really die? This was for a time the leading naturalistic theory – that Jesus merely swooned or fainted on the cross; revived himself in the tomb; rolled the massive stone away sealing his tomb; somehow slipped past the Roman soldiers guarding the tomb and then convinced his followers that he had risen from the dead when, in fact, he had only fainted. The practical impossibility of this theory reminds me of the story of the boy who submitted the following letter to a question-and-answer forum of a magazine:

> Dear Sirs, regarding Easter my teacher says that Jesus just swooned on the cross and that the disciples nursed him back to health. What do you think? Sincerely, Tommy.

The reply was:

> Dear Tommy, I suggest you take your teacher and beat him, hard, 39 times with a cat-of nine-tails whip, then nail him to a cross, and hang him in the sun for six hours, then run a spear through his side into his lungs and put him in an airless tomb for 36 hours, and see what happens.

The swoon theory, though it was once popular, has been thoroughly discredited in modern times as going against the weight of historical evidence (including what we know about the thoroughness with which Roman soldiers made sure their crucified criminals really were dead; otherwise they might have ended up dead themselves) and modern medical knowledge (including the way in which the flow of blood and water from Jesus' side indicates that the spear would have pierced both Jesus' heart and lungs, the water indicative of a build-up of pericardial and pleural fluid in the membranes around the heart and lungs, itself a symptom of severe blood loss and thirst).

If the disciples were neither deceived nor deceivers, then perhaps they were just deluded. The third option. Some have tried to argue this, the leading alternative theory being that the disciples halluci-nated Jesus' resurrection.

Obviously, a hallucination theory could explain how it is possible that certain people would individually believe that they had seen someone come back from the dead. However, the problem with this theory is that even though it could account for appearances to individuals, it can't account for Jesus' appearances to groups because hallucinations are not a group phenomenon – particularly hallucinations that stay around for forty days, that over 500 people see, that talk and eat with groups of people and whose words and actions are afterwards remembered by different people in the exact same way.

It is the absence of any plausible naturalistic explanation for the agreed facts of history concerning the resurrection claim that has contributed to the important conclusion proposed in Oxford professor Swinburne's book, *The Resurrection of God Incarnate*. Applying the Bayes's Theorem probability analysis, Swinburne argues that a reasonable case can be made that it is 97 per cent probable that Jesus Christ really did rise from the dead. Of course, you can always find a book somewhere to support just about any claim you want, but here is a book published by Oxford University Press and peer-reviewed at the highest levels of academia. Admittedly, as Swinburne himself has said, we shouldn't make too much of the exact number he arrives at as a percentage, as with any conclusion in probability theory, his calculation is based at various points on educated estimates that are plugged into the equation; but the emphasis is on the word 'educated'. The fact that Swinburne can ably defend his conclusion at academic conferences all around the world speaks to the fact that there is a substantial body of supporting reasons and historical evidence for the resurrection of Jesus Christ that cannot simply be ignored. Yet, that is exactly what many commentators, who make dismissive claims about belief in an historical resurrection, often do.

Famous British scholar N. T. Wright states:

> I have examined all the alternative explanations, ancient and modern, for the rise of the early church, and I have to say that far and away the best historical explanation is that Jesus of Nazareth . . . really did rise from the dead.

Even Géza Vermes, a sceptical scholar, admitted that no naturalistic explanations have been offered in 2,000 years of historical inquiry that can satisfactorily account for the agreed facts of history: that is, the disciples' sincere claims to have experienced the risen Jesus, the complete transformation of their lives and worldviews and the quick growth of the early Church. That is why the approach of those who deny the resurrection seems to have shifted in the last couple of decades, from an attempt to use historical research to falsify the resurrection to the assertion that the historical question of the resurrection 'is probably unanswerable'.

But in history, as in a court of law, the evidence demands a verdict. Provided one approaches the evidence without any prior dogmatic presuppositions with regard to miracles, the explanation that makes best sense of these remarkable and agreed facts of history is that Jesus Christ really and truly rose from the dead. In fact, it is not just that it is the *best* explanation – in the sense that it best fits the facts. It is also the *only* explanation that fits the facts.

No wonder then, that there exists a large number of well publicized testimonies of former sceptical lawyers, philosophers, scientists, detectives and journalists, all of whom became convinced of the validity of the resurrection in the very process of investigating Christianity in order to disprove it: people such as Simon Greenleaf, C. S. Lewis, Frank Morrison, John Warwick Montgomery, Alister McGrath, Lee Strobel and J. Warner Wallace. Their work highlights that with respect to much of the ongoing popular scepticism towards Christianity's historical claims, it is not so much that the evidence has been investigated and found wanting, it is that the evidence has so often not been investigated at all.

The significance of the resurrection

The significance of the resurrection of Jesus Christ as an historical fact cannot be overstated, for we are normally told that when we die, that's it. Game over. That our lives – all that we are: our thoughts, emotions and memories – simply cease to be. Ashes to ashes. Dust to dust. The contemporary French philosopher Luc Ferry says this:

> As distinct from the animals, a human being is the only creature who . . . knows that he will die and that those he loves will also die. Consequently, he cannot prevent himself from thinking about this state of affairs, which is disturbing and absurd, almost unimaginable.

No wonder the famous artist Damian Hirst writes:

> Why do I feel so important when I'm not? Nothing is important and everything is important. I do not know why I am here, but I am glad that I am. I'd rather be here than not. I am going to die and I want to live forever, I can't escape that fact, and I can't let go of that desire.

For all of us, death is the great inevitable, hanging over our lives like a spectre, threatening to rob the present of any meaning that could possibly transcend the finitude of our lives, and filling us with fear the closer we get to it. The significance of the resurrection of Jesus Christ, however, is that – if true – death does not have to have the final say over our lives. Because it means that Jesus not only took all our moral brokenness, our guilt and our shame on his shoulders as he hung on the cross, and buried these things in the grave as he died; he also defeated death – not just metaphorically, but literally, which means that all who put their trust in him no longer need to fear death.

The wonder of all this, for me, is not just the beauty of the story of a God who would give his life for ours, and eventually triumph over our greatest enemy – death. It is also that there is no reason for the story to be relegated to the realm of myth, fairy tale or wishful thinking. For, as we have seen, it's a story, based on reality, rooted in the historical life, death and resurrection of the person of Jesus Christ, and completely open to investigation by those who are willing to grapple with the evidence in the pursuit of truth.

And what could be better than a good story than a story that is both good and true?

10

Conclusion

World without soul

I really enjoy hearing about people's different faith journeys. Everyone's story is unique.

Recently, I read a fascinating interview with *New York Times* columnist David Brooks about his journey. Brooks recalls: 'I grew up in a more or less secular world and its categories were my assumptions.' But as he got older, experienced more of life and paid more attention to the many people he had the privilege to meet and write about, he said:

> [I]t didn't make sense to me that they were just sacks of genetic material. It only made sense to me that they had *souls*. That there was some piece of them that had no material dimension, no size or shape but gave them infinite dignity, every single one of them.

As Brooks explains, it was this realization that helped him to see 'various glimpses of another layer of life', and over time, his perspective shifted. He adds:

> I went from a very clear nonbeliever to somebody who felt belief was good for others but that it didn't really impact me; and then to a growing awareness which felt more like recognizing something that was latent in me, that I actually do have belief.

Looking back on his younger self, he therefore concludes: 'My mental categories were inadequate to reality as I experienced it.' In other words, his secular or atheistic assumptions didn't quite work in the real world of people and relationships. They weren't able to explain the complexity and depth of human life or the textures and hues of the world he experienced, in the way he eventually discovered Christianity could.

Christian faith makes sense of the things that really matter to a human soul: meaning and purpose, value and goodness, truth and love, as well as hope in the midst of suffering. This is something the atheist position struggles to do, for its chief method of explanation is reductionism; sometimes referred to as 'nothing buttery'. Why? Because it ultimately reduces those things key to our human experience – such as meaning and morality or friendship and love – to 'nothing but' physics and chemistry, 'nothing but' genetics and DNA or 'nothing but' the brain and its neurons in operation.

Christianity makes sense of the operation of physics, chemistry, DNA and the workings of the human brain in human life; but in contrast to the reductionism of atheism, it also holds that a human life is more than these things. Just as art is more than splashes of paint on a canvas and music more than a combination of sounds, Christianity maintains that a human life is more than merely the sum of its physical parts.

The New Atheists may continue to laugh at the idea of the supernatural. Their world, as Daniel Dennett dismissively states, is a world without 'spooks'. But as we have seen, it is also a world without soul.

How does atheism explain our innate religious impulse as human beings – our hunger for the sacred, the spiritual? According to research by the University of Oxford's Centre of Anthropology and Mind, human thought is intractably linked to religious concepts such as the existence of God, supernatural agents and the possibility of an afterlife. Moreover, according to an article in *New Scientist* magazine, a lot of studies by cognitive scientists suggest that atheism as a belief is actually psychologically impossible because of the way humans are wired to think. In other words, according to cognitive science, atheists don't really believe what they say they believe. Ironically, the author of that article, Dr Graham Lawton, is an avowed atheist himself.

As the inventor, Thomas Edison, famously observed, 'human beings are incurably religious'.

Some atheist thinkers have tried to explain our spiritual longings and religious impulses as a biological survival mechanism, that is, 'nothing but' a desire or impulse brought about by our genes because our genes recognize that such an impulse will in some measure enhance our chances of survival as a species.

This explanation, however, raises all sorts of problematic questions: how is it possible that our genes, which are a part of us, are so much smarter than the whole of us – in that they are able to trick us into believing what they want us to believe, simply for their own purposes of continued survival? Is it only atheists who can transcend their genes to know when their genes are trying to trick them? And if so, how have atheists achieved this feat while religious people have been unable to do so? And if the answer is on the basis of reason, how can atheists be sure that all their reasoned conclusions are true, if all our thoughts are ultimately controlled by our genes whose primary motive is not truth, but evolutionary success?

In contrast to the 'nothing buttery' of atheistic reductionism, Lewis reasons that 'if I find in myself a desire which no experience in this world can satisfy, the most probable explanation is that I was made for another world.'

The Christian story of reality makes sense of the depth and complexity of human experience, and yet you only need to pick up a book from New Atheist writers such as Dennett or Dawkins, and you will see how they confidently lambast belief in God as 'insane', 'deluded', 'demented', 'irrational' or 'outdated'. Why? Is it because atheism has inspired humanity's best thoughts throughout the ages? No. Is it because they have offered the world a reasoned and evidence-based account of how atheism, above all other belief systems, is best equipped to answer life's fundamental questions? No. Or is it because they have finally demonstrated that reality does not have a spiritual dimension? No.

According to philosopher James K. A. Smith, the actual appeal of the New Atheists is the promise of 'status' and 'respectability', more than the promise of 'an adequate explanation'. Smith argues that people 'buy in' to the New Atheist position – 'less because the "system" works intellectually and more because it comes with an allure of illumination and sophistication'. It offers *belonging*, the opportunity to be in the circle of those 'in the know' – the enlightened ones.

But in their attempt to distinguish between the enlightened ones, who base their lives on reason, and the deluded ones, who base their life on faith, the New Atheists fail to realize that both reason and faith are essential to a sane life. The question is not whether or not to believe in anything. The question is what to believe in and why.

In actual fact, our reason itself is a matter of faith. As Chesterton explains: 'It is an act of faith to assert that our thoughts have any relation to reality at all.'

A faith that makes sense

As we have seen, Christian faith is not hostile to reason, nor reason to Christian faith. Indeed, Christianity gives us a reason to put faith in our reasoning in a way that atheism does not. For if everything, including our minds, is nothing more than the product of natural, unguided, mindless processes – as atheism tends to suggest – on what rational basis can we assume that reality is intelligible; and on what basis can we assume that our minds are giving us a true account of that reality?

As Einstein once remarked: 'The most incomprehensible thing about the world is that it is comprehensible.' But it is only incomprehensible from an atheistic perspective. From the Christian perspective, the intelligibility of the universe makes complete sense because there is an intelligence behind it all – an 'orderer' behind the order and a designer behind the design. When reality is viewed from a Christian point of view, rationality makes sense; the discipline of science makes sense with all its scientific discoveries; the existence of right and wrong and of good and evil makes sense; and the depth and complexity of our human experience makes sense – including our deepest longings and desires.

Christianity is a faith that works in the real world because it makes sense of this real world. There's no need for those who put their faith in Jesus Christ to suspend simultaneously their reason, intellect or love of science. Indeed, Christianity is an eminently sane belief in that it makes sense not only of the realm of the intellect and reason, but of all the other human faculties as well, including our emotions, intuitions and imagination.

Although New Atheists like to describe Christian faith as a sort of deluded imagination bordering on insanity, Chesterton suggests it is not imagination that causes insanity, but the lack of it. He writes: 'The madman is not the man who has lost his reason; the mad man is the man who has lost everything except his reason.'

The point is that reason is essential to sanity but not sufficient. We need imagination also, for reason is a valuable tool, but not a productive one. It is mainly a weapon of defence. It tests propositions, one proposition after another; but it takes imagination to attempt to see the big picture, to draw the disparate strands together as a whole, to apprehend the meaning buried beneath the surface of things.

I find it fascinating that many of the greatest advances in scientific knowledge – those of Copernicus, Newton, Pasteur, Einstein – involved vast leaps of the imagination. This aspect of science is most famously captured by Einstein himself who said: 'I am enough of an artist to draw freely upon my imagination. Imagination is more important than knowledge. Knowledge is limited. Imagination encircles the world.'

Let me ask you, dear reader: is it beyond the realm of your imagination that behind all that you can see with your eyes, there is a God who made you, who loves you and who longs for you to know and experience his grace: his acting in your life, your thoughts, your feelings and in your heart?

I don't know if you have ever paused to consider why it is that we care about the things we have been talking about in this book in the first place – meaning, value, goodness, truth, love, suffering and hope – or how unlikely or unnatural it would be for us to care about the question of God or of life after death, if there really were no God or life after death.

According to the Bible, God 'has put eternity' in the hearts of men and women (Ecclesiastes 3.11, KJV). As King Solomon observes, this is a soul-deep longing that can be squashed or distracted, but never wholly diverted by romance, wealth, fame, pleasure or success. It's like an internal homing beacon, faint but persistent, easily drowned out by competing noises, but always there in the background, waiting for us to listen, calling us home.

We see this dimension of the human condition brilliantly illuminated in one of the great works of literature, Augustine's *Confessions*, the first autobiography in recorded history. In it, we learn of the precocious young Augustine's journey from a belief in the God of the Bible to a rejection of his childhood faith and a search for satisfaction in pleasure and success; from a place of adult success and accomplishment to a philosophical search for answers to life's deepest questions and, finally, from a place of profound philosophical questioning back to Christian faith – but this time, a faith now tested in the crucible of reason and experience.

In the most famous line from that book, Augustine memorably illustrates the human predicament as follows: 'You have made us for yourself, O Lord, and our hearts are restless, until they rest in you.'

Homelessness and home

Restlessness, that sense of never quite being at home in the world, is a theme that almost every person on the planet can relate to – particularly in the West where our lives are often characterized by busyness, instability and change.

The journalist Malcolm Muggeridge, who late in life came to Christian faith, states:

> The first thing I remember about the world – and I pray it may be the last – is that I was a stranger in it. The feeling which everyone has to some degree, and which is at once the glory and desolation of homo sapiens, provides the only thread of consistency that I can see in my life.

Chesterton, expressing the same sentiment, writes in a poem entitled 'The house of Christmas': 'For men are homesick in their own homes / And strangers under the sun'. But like Augustine and Muggeridge, the feeling does not lead Chesterton to despair, for he recognizes that there is a home for the human soul, though not one found in any particular place.

As the rest of his poem reads:

> . . . For men are homesick in their own homes,
> And strangers under the sun . . .
> But our homes are under miraculous skies
> Where the yule tale was begun.
>
> A Child in a foul stable,
> Where the beasts feed and foam;
> Only where He was homeless
> Are you and I at home;
> We have hands that fashion and heads that know,

But our hearts we lost – how long ago!
In a place no chart nor ship can show
Under the sky's dome . . .

To an open house in the evening
Home shall men come,
To an older place than Eden
And a taller town than Rome.
To the end of the way of the wandering star,
To the things that cannot be and that are,
To the place where God was homeless
And all men are at home.

Jesus Christ, the Son of God, left his home in heaven in order to draw us home to himself. Augustine asks: 'Could God have done anything kinder or more generous than for the real, eternal, unchanging wisdom of God itself . . . to condescend to take on human form?'

He was born in a dirty stable to a Jewish peasant girl. He was brought up in an obscure village on the eastern fringe of the Roman Empire. He sweated at a carpenter's bench to support his mother and younger siblings. Eventually, he began his ministry of teaching, healing and proclaiming the good news that life in the kingdom of God was available for all. He had few possessions and no home – no place to rest his head. He travelled on foot, ministering from village to village. Those who followed him were plain and earthy folk, mainly fishermen and the like. He made friends with prostitutes and publicans, and laid hands on lepers and outcasts.

He scandalized the religious leaders of the day by dining with sinners and pronouncing forgiveness of sin. So, they tested him, misrepresented him and tried earnestly to discredit him. Almost all those in power saw him as a nuisance and a threat. Still some, risking their reputations, put their hope and trust in him.

But in the end, he was arrested, and all his followers fled. He was tried as a criminal, and although the Roman Governor, Pontius Pilate, recognized that he was an innocent man, he was sentenced to be flogged and nailed to a cross to die.

He didn't protest, nor curse, as they spat in his face and pulled out his beard, lacerated his back and crowned his head with thorns. As the cruel nails were driven into his hands and feet, and as they lifted the cross to the sky, he cried, 'Father, forgive them, for they do not know what they are doing' (Luke 23.34, NIV).

And yet, his death was not a tragedy but a victory. It was not the frustration of his mission but the accomplishment of it. For, having assumed our nature, as a human being, Jesus also assumed, on the cross, all our guilt and shame and bore the punishment for all our sins.

And when it was all done and paid for, Jesus cried out: 'It is finished.' And died. For us.

At the heart of Christian faith is not a set of beliefs per se but an event: the crucifixion of Jesus Christ, the Son of God. An historical event, with cosmic repercussions. An unthinkable event, in light of our pretensions to self-sufficiency, yet one that speaks to our deepest hungers and fears. An event that calls us back to humility and with it, hope.

The Bible says: 'God so loved the world that he gave his one and only Son, that whoever believes in him shall not perish but have eternal life' (John 3.16, NIV).

Isn't it wonderful to think that God loves the world that much – that he loves *you* that much?

God loves you. The Bible is 100 per cent clear about the fact that he sent his Son into the world to rescue broken people – including me and you – and that he invites us to be reconciled to him, in our heart of hearts. To return to him. To come home.

But he will never force our hand. Why not? Because that would deprive us of precisely the good that he intends for us, which is to restore our spiritually dead hearts to *Life*. 'I have come that they may have life,' said Jesus, 'and have it to the full' (John 10.10, NIV). But you can't bring a spiritually dead heart to life by force.

Remember Augustine's quote: 'You have made us for yourself, O Lord, and our hearts are restless until they rest in you.' If Christ tried to make us come to him by force, our hearts would still be restless because we wouldn't be resting, we would be resisting.

Kingdoms in conflict

The Life that Christ calls us to is found in a freely given and freely received, interactive living relationship with God and his kingdom. (The Bible says: 'Now this is eternal life: that they know you, the only true God, and Jesus Christ whom you have sent', John, 17.3, NIV.) But we can't experience that Life unless we are willing to receive Christ and step into God's kingdom, and we can't step into God's kingdom unless we are willing to let go of our own kingdom.

And that is both the easiest and the most difficult thing in the world for us to do.

For God's kingdom, as Dallas Willard puts it, is the range of his effective will, where what he wants done is done, whereas our kingdom is the range of our effective will, where what we want done is done.

Our kingdoms start off small. For our first child, Grace, it all began with the discovery of her right index finger. She was about five or six months old, and this incredible discovery fascinated her for days. This thing she could hold in front of her face and bend, if she wanted, or straighten, if she wanted. The intoxicating thing for her was that it was something *she* could control, direct, decide. Because it was *her* finger.

Eventually, she discovered her others fingers as well, followed by her legs and her voice, and each time, as she made those first little choices about what she would do with her hands, feet and voice, my wife and I would say to each other: 'Look at what she did!' Or: 'Did you hear what she just said?'

We so cherished and valued her creativity and individuality. Why? Because this is what makes her more than just a thing. The glory of us human beings is that we have the ability to make genuine choices. This is part of what it means to be made in God's image: that we don't just act on pure animal instinct or biological impulse or according to fate. As human beings, we have the capacity to create or to bring something new into this universe, each time we make a choice. Each time we make a decision. Because it is from our heart or will that we make our choices. And it is from our heart that we decide the most important thing of all: what we love.

From the Bible's perspective, the most destiny-defining thing about you is what you choose to love above all else, for that is what your kingdom is built on. It doesn't take us very long as little children to discover that we have a kingdom. It may start with a single finger, but over the years that kingdom grows.

For example, what are a two-year old's favourite words? 'No' and 'mine'. These are important words. Kingdom words. Words that are about defining the realm of where what we say goes, asserting our will.

Our ability to choose is precious, but it is also a problem because our will is not the only reality in the universe. So, what happens when our will runs into something else that doesn't want to cooperate – like a toy that runs out of batteries? Or, *someone* else who doesn't want to cooperate – like a brother or a sister?

Did you grow up with a sibling? If so, can you remember the first thing two kids often do when they get in the back seat of their parents' car? They draw a line down the middle and say to each other: 'Don't cross that line.' They are learning about their kingdoms. And then, what happens next? They start crossing the line, invading the other's kingdom, so they bicker and fight. And then dad, if he's driving the car, gets upset because, of course, he thinks of the vehicle as *his* kingdom.

And there, in the car's microcosm, we have a picture of our problem: our little kingdoms, as we try to expand them, come into contact with obstacles that get in our way, including other little kingdoms. And then what do we have? Kingdoms in conflict.

Britain used to be a place of kingdoms in conflict, as the many castles and fortresses, dotted throughout the land, attest. Thankfully, that is a thing of the past and things are now relatively ordered and civil. But scratch just a bit beneath the surface, and you will soon see our civilized society is a thin veneer over fiercely competing wills.

Have you ever noticed that the newspapers are full of strife, violence, gossip and heartache every day? Without fail. You would think, maybe once or twice a year we might get a day when the newspapers have none of these things to report. Yet, so far, that day has not come, and in all likelihood, it never will.

We live in a world of kingdoms in conflict. That's the human condition. It is why we have all been hurt by other people, just as we have hurt others. That's how things are. That's what we are like.

In a way, we are all like individual ships trying to navigate our way through life while sharing the same ocean. We would love to be able to sail however, wherever, with whoever and whenever we want. Our aim is to pursue what we think makes us happy: whether it be *pleasure* (finding our own paradise island) or *fame* (being recognized wherever we go – 'Oh, there goes the HMS *Celebrity*!') or *relationships* (hanging out with the cool ships) or *status* (becoming known as a great ship) or *power* (capturing or dominating other ships) or *wealth* (becoming a trade ship or seeking buried treasure) or *beauty* (having the best-looking ship – 'Wow, check out the curves on those sails!'). You get the idea.

Like ships, we set sail for that which we love, that which we value as an ultimate good. But the problem is twofold: first, the ocean of life isn't always predictable. At times, it is smooth sailing, but at other times, the wind and the waves can threaten to overwhelm us. Second, there are lots of other ships in the sea, and they, too, have their telescopes set on the things that they want. And sometimes, what other sailors pursue gets in the way of the things we pursue because we both want the same thing.

And when that happens, what do we do? We either get the cannons out and attack the other boat; or we grab the ship's wheel and withdraw to avoid a collision. These two responses – attack and withdrawal – tend to characterize human relationships.

We attack people when we intentionally try to hurt them, dominate them, intimidate or undermine them, either physically or verbally; and we withdraw from people when we distance ourselves from them. We give them the silent treatment, or we literally just walk out on them.

These little battles get fought every day by people who work in the same business or charity, between players in same sporting team or between people who live in shared housing. Between people who are meant to be brothers and sisters, between husbands and wives, between parents and children.

And this is one of the reasons why our lives are characterized by stress and anxiety: we are torn between the competing emotions of fear and desire. We desire the things out there in life's ocean that we want and that we think will make us happy. But we fear anything that could sink our ship if we venture out into the ocean to get them. We fear the other ships in the sea and what they can do to us, and we fear the reality of life's uncertain circumstances on the high seas – storms, currents, icebergs – the unpredictable dangers of real life.

But surely this is not the way things were meant to be.

The adventure of faith

Leo Tolstoy, perhaps the world's greatest novelist, diagnoses the problem like this. He observes that each person is a natural egoist, who sees the world as if it were a novel in which he or she were the hero or heroine, but the 'truly good life' begins when a person can see the world as if he or she were a minor character in someone else's novel.

The Bible echoes this sentiment. It says that we weren't meant to live a life of fear in our own little kingdom, in our own little boat, in our own little story. It says we were meant to live in a much bigger story. A much bigger kingdom. In God's kingdom. In God's story.

In other words, something you need to realize about life is that it's not about you.

It's about me! Just kidding. The Bible says it is neither about you nor me; it's about God. This world is his world. He made it. He loves it. He owns it. And we have just gone and made a mess of it. A real mess. We are rebels setting up our little castles in somebody else's kingdom. But the castles that we think will bring us freedom actually become our own lonely little prisons, which is about as good a description of hell as you can possibly get.

So, what happens if you choose to stop living for yourself as the hero of the story and to start living for God, as part of his story where he is the hero? Well, it's kind of like this. Instead of living a life of attacking other boats with your cannons or sailing off to some lonely island cove, hoping no one, not even the winds or the waves, will bother you, you hear a voice. It is Jesus' voice. This is what he says: 'Get out of the boat! Get out of your little boat, it is floating on my ocean anyway. Get out of the boat, put your hand in mine and I will show you how to walk on water. How to live a supernatural life of love in which you rely entirely on me to keep you afloat. It's a life of faith and freedom, risk and adventure – but there's no safer place in the world to be.'

As I said, it is both the easiest and the hardest thing in the world to do. It is the hardest thing to do because you have to surrender, everything, to Jesus and trust him that he knows best. But it is also the easiest thing to do because all you have to do is *surrender*. Let go. Allow Christ to be the one who directs and manages your life.

Lewis writes:

The terrible thing, the almost impossible thing, is to hand over your whole self – all your wishes and precautions – to Christ. But it is far easier than what we are trying to do instead. For what we are trying to do is to remain what we call 'ourselves', to keep personal happiness as our great aim in life, and yet at the same time be 'good'. We are all trying to let our mind and heart go their own way – centred on money or pleasure or ambition – and hoping, in spite of this, to behave honestly and chastely and humbly.

And that is exactly what Christ warned us you could not do. As He said, a thistle cannot produce figs. If I am a field that contains nothing but grass-seed, I cannot produce wheat. Cutting the grass may keep it short: but I shall still produce grass and no wheat. If I want to produce wheat, the change must go deeper than the surface. I must be ploughed up and re-sown.

Letting go of your own little kingdom, where you call the shots, and stepping into God's kingdom, where he calls the shots, sounds scary. But it is worth it. And that's because knowing Jesus is the best thing in the world, simply because he himself is the best thing in the world: the source and centre of all that is good and beautiful and true. Your heart's true home.

As we come towards the end of this book, I cannot help but finish with something of a personal message to you, the reader. I do not believe it is an accident that this book came to be in your hands. And I certainly hope that it has helped you to see that the Christian faith does make sense – both to the head and the heart – and that trusting in Jesus Christ is the most sensible, rational and wonderful thing anyone could possibly do. But I would also not quite feel satisfied, for your sake, if that were as far as things went. That is, if your journey towards Christian faith only went as far as cognitive recognition of certain truths. For, at the end of the day, following Jesus is something you do. It is an adventure of faith. Scary, sure. But a perfectly reasonable faith, nonetheless.

Normally, and naturally, this adventure of faith begins by talking to God (which is prayer) and telling him that you want to follow him; that you are sorry for living life without him; that you are thankful for all that Jesus has done for you through his death and resurrection; that you accept his invitation to forgiveness and new life in relationship with him and that you are no longer living for your kingdom but living for his.

And the adventure begins . . . Each day learning from the Creator of life how to live. Learning from the one who really knows what life is meant to be and how to live it well. Learning how to look to him for my meaning and purpose; knowing his plans for me are good. Learning how to value myself not for what I do, but for who I am and whose I am. Learning to trust not in my own goodness, but his, and to draw on his grace to help me live as I was made to live. Learning to be still and listen to his voice, his guidance, his take on truth and on what it is that really matters. Learning to love not just those who are loveable, but also those who seem unlovable and undeserving to me. Just as Christ loved me. And learning to trust him even through times of suffering and pain, knowing he under-stands and is with me; and will never forsake me.

My hope and prayer for you is that you, too, will come to know and experience this life of adventure and love that comes through faith in Jesus Christ, if you haven't already. That you, too, will come to know, in the depths of your heart, that your life matters. That you are not here by accident, but here on purpose because God wanted you to be here. And that he wants the best possible life for you – not just for this life, but for life everlasting.

Bibliography

Ahbel-Rappe, Sara and Kamtekar, Rachana (eds) (2009) *A Companion to Socrates* (Oxford: Wiley-Blackwell).

Alexander, Brian and Young, Larry (2012) *The Chemistry Between Us: Love, sex and the science of attraction* (London: Current).

Alston, William P. (2002) 'What Euthyphro should have said', in William Lane Craig (ed.), *Philosophy of Religion: A reader and guide* (Edinburgh: Edinburgh University Press).

Andrews, Edgar (2012) *Who Made God?* (Darlington: EP Books).

Ariely, D. (2012) *The (Honest) Truth about Dishonesty* (New York: HarperCollins).

Beauvoir, Simone de (1949) *The Second Sex* (London: Penguin).

Ben-Shahar, Tal (2008) *Happier* (New York: McGraw-Hill).

Botton, Alain de (2005) *Status Anxiety* (London: Penguin).

Brian, D. (1996) *Einstein: A life* (New York: Wiley).

Carson, D. A. (2012) *The Intolerance of Tolerance* (Grand Rapids, MI: Eerdmans).

Chesterton, G. K. (1901) *The Defendant* (London: R. Brimley Johnson).

Chesterton, G. K. (2007) *The Everlasting Man* (Mineola, NY: Dover).

Chesterton, G. K. (1996) *Orthodoxy* (London: Hodder & Stoughton).

Chesterton, G. K. (1943) *St Thomas Aquinas* (London: Hodder & Stoughton).

Charles Darwin, Paul H. Barrett and R. B. Freeman (1992) *The Works of Charles Darwin, Vol. 16: The Origin of Species, 1876* (London: Routledge).

Dawkins, Richard (2001) *River Out of Eden* (London: Phoenix).

Dawkins, Richard (2016) *The God Delusion* (London: Black Swan).

Davies, Paul (1987) *The Cosmic Blueprint* (London: Heinemann).

D'Costa, G. (1996) *Resurrection Reconsidered* (Oxford: Oneworld Publications).

Dickson, John (2008) *A Spectator's Guide to World Religions* (Oxford: Lion Hudson).

Dickson, John (2019) *Is Jesus History?* (Epsom: Good Book Company).

Doyle, Arthur C. (1994) *The Sign of Four* (New York: Quality Paperback Book Club).

Dworkin, Ronald (2011) *Justice for Hedgehogs* (Cambridge, MA: Belknap Press of Harvard University Press).

Ehrman, Bart (2012) *The New Testament* (Oxford: Oxford University Press).

Einstein, A. and Harris, A. (1935) *The World as I See It* (London: John Lane).

Eldredge, J. (2001) *Wild at Heart: Discovering the* secret of a man's soul (Nashville, TN: Thomas Nelson).

Exell, J. (1886) *The Biblical Illustrator* (London: Fleming H. Revell Company)

Ferry, Luc (2011) *A Brief History of Thought* (New York: Harper Perennial).

Finnis, John (2011) *Natural Law and Natural Rights* (Oxford: Oxford University Press).

Frankl, V. (2004) *Man's Search for Meaning* (London: Ebury).

Gray, John (2002) *Straw Dogs: Thoughts on humans and other animals* (London: Granta).

Grimm, Robert (ed.) (2002) *Notable American Philanthropists* (London: Greenwood Press).

Greenleaf, S. (1847) *An examination of the testimony of the four evangelists by the rules of evidence administered in courts of justice [electronic resource] : With an account of the trial of Jesus* (2nd edition, revised and corrected by the author ed., Making of modern law, London: A. Maxwell.)

Gumbel, N. (2003) *Alpha Questions of Life: An opportunity to explore the meaning of life* (Colorado Springs, CO: Cook Communications Ministries).

Habermas, Gary R. and Licona, Michael R. (2004) *The Case for the Resurrection of Jesus* (Grand Rapids, MI: Kregel Publications).

Haldane J. B. S. (1965) 'Data needed for a blueprint of the first organism', in S. W. Fox (ed.) *The Origins of Prebiological Systems and their Molecular Matrices* (New York: Academic Press), p. 11.

Hardenberg, F. von (1888) *Hymns and Thoughts on Religion by Novalis*, Hastie, W. (trans.) (Edinburgh: T. & T. Clark).

Harris, Sam (2010) *The Moral Landscape: How science can determine human values* (London: Bantam).

Holland, Tom (2020) *Dominion: The making of the Western mind* (London: Abacus).

Hume, David and Buckle, S. (2007) *An Enquiry Concerning Human Understanding and Other Writings* (Cambridge Texts in the History of Philosophy) (Cambridge: Cambridge University Press).

Huxley, Aldous (1937) *Ends and Means* (London: Harper & Brothers Publishers).

Jami, Criss (2015) *Killosophy* (Scotts Valley, CA: CreateSpace).

Kreeft, Peter (1988) *Fundamentals of the Faith: Essays in Christian apologetics* (San Francisco, CA: Ignatius Press).

Lasch, Christopher and Lasch-Quinn, Elizabeth (1997) *Women and the Common Life : Love, marriage, and feminism* (New York: W. W. Norton).

Lecky, W. (1930) *History of European Morals from Augustus to Charlemagne* (London: Watts & Co.).

Lewis, C. S. (1972) *God in the Dock* (Grand Rapids, MI: William B. Eerdmans). Extracts quoted by permission. *God in the Dock* by C. S. Lewis © CS Lewis Pte Ltd 1970.

Lewis, C. S. (1940) *The Problem of Pain* (London: Geoffrey Bles). Extract quoted by permission. *The Problem of Pain* by C. S. Lewis © CS Lewis Pte Ltd 1940.

Lewis, C. S. (1955) *Surprised by Joy* (London: Geoffrey Bles). Extract

quoted by permission. *Surprised by Joy* by C. S. Lewis © CS Lewis
Pte Ltd 1955.

Lewis, C. S. (2011) *Mere Christianity* (New York: HarperCollins).
Extracts quoted by permission. *Mere Christianity* by C. S. Lewis
© CS Lewis Pte Ltd 1942, 1943, 1944, 1952.

Lewis, C. and Hooper, W. (1980) *The Weight of Glory, and Other
Addresses* (New York: Macmillan). Extract quoted by permission.
The Weight of Glory by C. S. Lewis © CS Lewis Pte Ltd 1949.

Lennox, John (2009) *God's Undertaker: Has Science Buried God?*
(Oxford: Lion).

Lennox, John (2011) *Gunning for God: Why the New Atheists are
missing the target* (Oxford: Lion).

Lévi-Strauss, Claude (1968) *Structural Anthropology* (London: Allen
Lane).

Lippmann, W. (2008) *Liberty and the News* (Princeton, NJ: Princeton
University Press).

Lloyd-Jones, Sally (2007) *The Jesus Storybook Bible* (Grand Rapids,
MI: Zondervan).

McGrath, Alister (2020) *Through a Glass Darkly: Journeys through
science, faith and doubt* (London: Hodder & Stoughton).

Mackie, J. L. (1982) *The Miracle of Theism* (Oxford: Clarendon Press).

Martínez, P. and Sims, A. (2018) *Mad or God?* (London: IVP).

Morison, F. (1983) *Who Moved the Stone?* (Bromley: STL).

Morgan, D. (2010) *The SPCK Introduction to Karl Barth* (London:
SPCK).

Montgomery, J. W. (2016) *Fighting the Good Fight* (Orlando, FL: Wipf
& Stock).

Muggeridge, M. and Hunter, I. (1998) *The Very Best of Malcolm
Muggeridge* (London: Hodder & Stoughton).

Nagel, Thomas (1997) *The Last Word* (Oxford: Oxford University
Press).

Newbigin, Lesslie (2014) *The Gospel in a Pluralist Society* (London:
SPCK).

Nietzsche, Friedrich (1911) *Twilight of the Idols* (New York: Macmillan).

Paley, William (2009) *Natural Theology* (Cambridge: Cambridge Library Collection).

Pascal, Blaise (2003) *The Mind on Fire: A faith for the skeptical and indifferent; from the writings of Blaise Pascal*, J. M. Houston (abr. and ed.) (Vancouver: Regent College Publishing).

Pascal, Blaise (2008) *Human Happiness* (London: Penguin).

Plato (2007) *The Republic* (London: Penguin Classics).

Russell, Bertrand (1923) *A Free Man's Worship* (Portland, ME: T. B. Mosher).

Russell, Bertrand (1976) *Mysticism and Logic* (Abingdon: Routledge).

Ruse, Michael and Mayr, E. (1982) *Darwinism Defended: A guide to the evolution controversies* (London: Addison-Wesley).

Sartre, J., and Mairet, P. (1973) *Existentialism and Humanism* (London: Eyre Methuen).

Scruton, Roger (1994) *Modern Philosophy* (London: Penguin).

Scruton, Roger (2014) *The Soul of the World* (Princeton, NJ: Princeton University Press).

Sheed, F. J. (1984) *The Confessions of St Augustine* (London: Sheed & Ward).

Skinner, B. F. (1974) *About Behaviorism* (New York: Vintage).

Smith, James K. A. (2019) *On the Road with Saint Augustine* (Grand Rapid, MI: Brazos Press).

Solzhenitsyn, A. (1972) '*One Word of Truth . . .': The Nobel speech on literature 1970* (London: Bodley Head).

Strobel, Lee (2016) *The Case for Christ* (Grand Rapids, MI: Zondervan).

Swinburne, R. (2003) *The Resurrection of God Incarnate* (Oxford: Oxford University Press).

Tolkien, J. R. R. (2012) *Lord of the Rings* (Boston, MA: Mariner).

Vermès, Geza (2008) *The Resurrection* (London: Penguin).

Warner-Wallace, J. *Cold-Case Christianity* (Colorado Springs, CO: David C. Cook).

Wicks, Robert (2014) *Kant: A complete introduction* (London: Hodder & Stoughton).

Willard, Dallas (2014) *The Allure of Gentleness: Defending the faith in the manner of Jesus* (San Francisco, CA: HarperOne).

Willard, Dallas (2014) *The Divine Conspiracy: Rediscovering our hidden life in God* (London: William Collins).

Willard, Dallas (2018) *The Disappearance of Moral Knowledge* (New York: Taylor & Francis).

Wolterstorff, Nicholas (1987) *Lament for a Son* (Grand Rapids, MI: William B. Eerdmans).

Wright, J. (2009) *Hume's 'A Treatise of Human Nature': An introduction* (Cambridge Introductions to Key Philosophical Texts) (Cambridge: Cambridge University Press).

Yancey, Philip (2010) *What Good Is God?* (London: Hodder & Stoughton).

Other printed and online sources

Adams, Candace (2000) 'Leading nanoscientist builds big faith', *Baptist Standard*, 15 March.

Al-Khalili, Jim (2012) 'What is love? Five theories on the greatest emotion of all', *The Guardian*, 13 December.

Ananthaswamy, Anil (2012) 'Is the universe fine-tuned for life?', *Nova*, 7 March (available online at: <https://pbs.org/wgbh/nova/article/is-the-universe-fine-tuned-for-life>, accessed December 2020).

Associated Press, The (1994) 'A Stradivarius lost 27 years ago now brings tug of war', *New York Times*, 23 October (available online at: <www.nytimes.com/1994/10/23/us/a-stradivarius-lost-27-years-now-brings-tug-of-war.html>, accessed December 2020).

Atheist bus campaign (available online at: <https://humanism.org.uk/campaigns/successful-campaigns/atheist-bus-campaign>, accessed December 2020).

BBC News (2000) 'What they said: Genome in quotes', *BBC News*, 26 June (available online at: <http://news.bbc.co.uk/1/hi/sci/tech/807126.stm>, accessed 11 December 2020).

Bort, Julie (2016) '"I've never felt more isolated": The man who sold Minecraft to Microsoft for $2.5 billion reveals the empty side of success', *The Independent*, 29 September (available online at: <www.independent.co.uk/life-style/gadgets-and-tech/i-ve-never-felt-more-isolated-man-who-sold-minecraft-microsoft-2-5-billion-reveals-empty-side-success-a7329146.html>, accessed December 2020).

Brodwin, Erin (2016) 'What psychology actually says about the tragically social media-obsessed society in "Black Mirror"', *Business Insider*, 26 October (available online at: <http://static1.businessinsider.com/psychology-black-mirror-nosedive-social-media-2016-10>, accessed December 2020).

Brooks, David (2014) 'What suffering does', *New York Times*, 7 April (available online at: <www.nytimes.com/2014/04/08/opinion/brooks-what-suffering-does.html>, accessed December 2020).

Chesterton, G. K. (2008) 'The house of Christmas', *The Chesterton Review*, 34(3), pp. 475–476.

Craig, Nicke and Snook, Scott A. (2014) 'From purpose to impact', *Harvard Business Review*, May (available online at: <https://hbr.org/2014/05/from-purpose-to-impact>, accessed December 2020).

Craig, William Lane (2006) 'Is there historical evidence for the resurrection of Jesus?', The Craig v. Ehrman Debate, March (available online at: <https://reasonablefaith.org/media/debates/is-there-historical-evidence-for-the-resurrection-of-jesus-the-craig-ehrman>, accessed December 2020).

Davies, Paul (2007) 'Yes, the universe looks like a fix. But that doesn't mean that a god fixed it', *The Guardian*, 26 June (available online at: <https://theguardian.com/commentisfree/2007/jun/26/spaceexploration.comment>, accessed December 2020).

Donnelly, Laura and Scott, Patrick (2017) 'Mental health crisis among children as selfie culture sees cases of anxiety rise by 42 per cent in five years, NHS figures show', *The Telegraph*, 22 January (available online at: <https://www.telegraph.co.uk/health-fitness/mind/mental-health-crisis-among-children-selfie-culture-sees-cases>, accessed December 2020).

Eames, Tom (2013) 'Nicole Kidman: "Oscar win showed me the emptiness of my life"', *Digital Spy*, 20 November (available online at: <www.digitalspy.com/movies/a532637/nicole-kidman-oscar-win-showed-me-the-emptiness-of-my-life>, accessed December 2020).

Einstein, Albert (1936) 'Physics and reality' in *Journal of the Franklin Institute,* 221(3), pp. 349–82.

Fry, Stephen 'How can I be happy?' (available online at: <https://youtu.be/Tvz0mmF6NW4>, accessed December 2020).

Gibbs, Nancy (2017) 'When a president can't be taken at his word', *Time Magazine*, 3 April (available online at: <https://time.com/4710615/donald-trump-truth-falsehoods>, accessed December 2020).

Habermas, Gary (2004), 'My pilgrimage from atheism to theism: a discussion between Antony Flew and Gary Habermas', *Philosophia Christi*, 6(2) (available online at: <https://digitalcommons.liberty.edu/cgi/viewcontent.cgi?article=1336&context=lts_fac_pubs>, accessed December 2020).

Halliday, Nigel (2012) 'Damien Hirst', *Third Way Magazine*, May (available online at: <https://thirdway.hymnsam.co.uk/editions/may-2012-/reviews/damien-hirst.aspx>, accessed December 2020).

Harris, Sam (2011) 'Toward a science of morality', *Huffington Post*, 7 June (available online at: <https://www.huffpost.com/entry/a-science-of-morality_b_567185?guccounter=1>, accessed December 2020).

Holland, Tom (2019) 'We swim in Christian waters', *Church Times*, 27 September (available online at: <www.churchtimes.co.uk/articles/2019/27-september/features/features/tom-holland-

interview-we-swim-in-christian-waters>, accessed December 2020).

Hoyle, Fred (1981) 'The universe: past and present reflections', *Engineering and Science,* 45(2), November (available online at: <http://calteches.library.caltech.edu/527/2/Hoyle.pdf>, accessed December 2020).

Lawton, Graham (2019) 'Why almost everyone believes in an afterlife – even atheists', *NewScientist*, 20 November (available online at: <https://newscientist.com/article/mg24432570-500-why-almost-everyone-believes-in-an-afterlife-even-atheists/#ixzz6g7zE2AzO>, accessed December 2020).

M'Naghten [1843] UKHL J16 House of Lords (see: <http://e-lawresources.co.uk/M%27Naghten.php>, accessed December 2020).

Nielsen, Kai (1984) 'Why should I be moral? Revisited', *American Philosophical Quarterly*, 21(1), pp. 81–91.

Pannenberg, W. (1998) 'The historical Jesus as a challenge to Christology', *Dialog*, 37(1), pp. 22–7.

Post-truth world, the, briefing (2016) 'Yes, I'd lie to you', *The Economist*, 10 September (available online at: <www.economist.com/briefing/2016/09/10/yes-id-lie-to-you>, accessed December 2020).

Scruton, Roger (2014) 'Humans' hunger for the sacred: Why can't the New Atheists understand that?', *The Spectator*, 31 May (available online at: <www.spectator.co.uk/article/humans-hunger-for-the-sacred-why-can-t-the-new-atheists-understand-that>, accessed December 2020).

Skiena, Steven and Ward, Charles B. (2013) 'Who's biggest? The 100 most significant figures in history', *Time Magazine*, 10 December (available online at: <https://ideas.time.com/2013/12/10/whos-biggest-the-100-most-significant-figures-in-history>, accessed December 2020).

#StatusofMind campaign (available online at: <www.rsph.org.uk/

our-work/campaigns/status-of-mind.html>, accessed December 2020).

Stewart, Naomi (2016) 'Swipe right for negative self-perception says research into Tinder users', *The Guardian*, 4 August (available online at: <https://theguardian.com/science/2016/aug/04/swipe-right-for-negative-self-perception-says-research-into-tinder-users>, accessed December 2020).

Wehner, Peter (2019) 'David Brooks's journey toward faith', *The Atlantic*, 7 May (available online at: <www.theatlantic.com/ideas/archive/2019/05/second-mountain-brooks-discusses-his-faith/588766>, accessed December 2020).

Wright, N. T. (2014) 'Only love believes: The resurrection of Jesus and the constraints of history', *ABC*, 17 April (available online at: <https://abc.net.au/religion/only-love-believes-the-resurrection-of-jesus-and-the-constraints/10099298>, accessed December 2020).

WE HAVE A VISION OF A WORLD IN WHICH EVERYONE IS TRANSFORMED BY CHRISTIAN KNOWLEDGE

As well as being an award-winning publisher, SPCK is the oldest Anglican mission agency in the world.

Our mission is to lead the way in creating books and resources that help everyone to make sense of faith.

Will you partner with us to put good books into the hands of prisoners, great assemblies in front of schoolchildren and reach out to people who have not yet been touched by the Christian faith?

To donate, please visit www.spckpublishing.co.uk/donate or call our friendly fundraising team on 020 7592 3900.